JAPANESE TANKS

AND ARMOURED WARFARE

1932-45

A MILITARY AND POLITICAL HISTORY

DAVID McCORMACK

FONTHILL

www.fonthill.media
books@fonthill.media

First published in the United Kingdom
and the United States of America 2021

British Library Cataloguing in Publication Data:
A catalogue record for this book is available from the British Library

ISBN 978-1-78155-810-2

Typeset in 10pt on 13pt Sabon
Printed and bound in England

*This book is dedicated to the memory of
Jake Handley, Graham Skeates, and Richie Donovan
who will be remembered as wonderful travelling companions and
keen students of history.*

Acknowledgements

There are several people who I must thank for helping this project to come to fruition. First and foremost is my amazing wife Jenny, whose patience, understanding, and unconditional support enables me to be who I am. I must also express my lasting gratitude to my good friends on both sides of the pond, especially Sharon Schollenberger who regularly gives up her valuable time to proofread my work, and Chuck Willard whose kindness, unstinting support, and enthusiasm has been an inspiration to me over the last few years. As this is a book about tanks and armoured warfare, I would like to thank my former mentor Professor Alaric Searle of the University of Salford whose support and advice has always been appreciated.

Contents

Introduction

When I first announced my intention to write a book about Japanese tanks and armoured warfare on social media, the response was interesting to say the least. It was certainly very gratifying to read the positive feedback from people, particularly those whose view of history remained largely Eurocentric. Having said that, it soon became clear to me that apart from the well-known example of the Malayan campaign, the employment of Japanese armour was not something which many of my prospective readers were particularly aware of. Indeed, for some, the notion of employing tanks in the jungles of Southeastern Asia or on far-flung Pacific atolls and islands sounded absurd.

To some degree, the perceptions about Japanese tanks voiced by people in response to my social media posts helped to shape my ideas as I set about writing. As I saw it, my task was to debunk some prevailing myths and to encourage my readers to reconsider long standing misconceptions regarding the development, manufacture, and deployment of Japanese tanks. The popular image of the Japanese Army during the Second World War is of fanatical officers leading suicidal banzai charges with their samurai swords in hand. This view of the noble yet fiercely savage Samurai warrior as an anachronism still prevails in the minds of many. Yet, the reality is that Japan was an advanced technological nation, albeit one that struggled to come to terms with the challenges this brought to a deeply traditional and conservative society.

Japan fought on several fronts against several different enemies between 1931 and 1945. As such, I have placed the design, development, production, and operational deployment of Japanese tanks within the context of the almost continuous strife in which the nation found itself embroiled. The seemingly endless, frustrating war in China and the chastening experience of coming up against superior Soviet armour in Manchuria should have informed future

Japanese tank design, doctrine, tactical and operational deployments, but misplaced national pride prevented rational development. Later, the mirage of success in the steaming Jungles of Malaya only served to reinforce the view of the Japanese that they knew all there was to know about modern armoured warfare.

As solid research serves to augment the authenticity of any new project, my first task was to locate good sources on Japanese tanks and armoured warfare in general. My first port of call was Alaric Searle's excellent 2017 book *Armoured Warfare: A Military, Political and Global History.* This book was particularly useful in terms of developing my thinking about the deployment of tanks in difficult terrain. Perhaps I am somewhat biased towards the author as he was my tutor for the Armoured Warfare module at the University of Salford when I was undertaking my BA in Contemporary Military and International History. In terms of secondary sources relating specifically to Japanese armour, I drew heavily on the works of Tomio Hara, Leland Ness, Paul M. Roland, Gordon L. Rottman, Akira Takizawa, and Stephen J. Zaloga. The primary resource material that I accessed came largely from American and Japanese memoirs, technical handbooks, reports, published letters, and archived magazines and newspapers.

Over the years, I have been fortunate enough to see some surviving examples of Japanese tanks. At the renowned Bovington Tank Museum, located in England's south-west county of Dorset, my attention has always been drawn towards the diminutive Ha-Go light tank which is dwarfed by some of the neighbouring exhibits. Further afield, my work as a battlefield tour guide has taken me to the excellent Kubinka Tank Museum located sixty-three kilometres west of Moscow. Here, I saw an absolutely first class collection of Japanese tanks and armoured fighting vehicles. At both sites my mind turned towards the crews of these tanks. How did they feel about being pitted against the mechanised might of America and the Soviet Union in their puny machines?

The historian C. V. Wedgewood once said that, 'Without the imaginative insight which goes with creative literature, history cannot be intelligently written.' As with my previous books, I have attempted to produce a history based on novelistic discourse rather than a dry recitation of facts and figures. As such, the focal point of my narrative is people, notably those who designed Japan's tanks, the thinkers who created the doctrine for their operation, the military commanders who committed them to action, and the crews who often fought unequal battles against vastly superior forces. A good history should be readable. By including the human element, I hope that I have achieved that.

David McCormack
Bear Cross, Bournemouth, Dorset, England.
March 2020

Prologue

During the early 1930s Japan was at the forefront of tank design and the innovative employment of combined-arms units. Yet despite establishing an early lead, these significant advantages never bore fruit as traditionalists in the Imperial Japanese Army (IJA) insisted that tanks should only be employed in an infantry support role. Meanwhile, in the west, theorists such as Jean Baptiste Eugéne Estienne, Heinz Guderian and Mikhail Tukhachevsky became highly influential, not only in their respective countries, but also internationally. Back in Japan, visionaries such as Tomio Hara discovered that attracting the attention of the conservative military establishment was much more problematical. As a consequence, Japanese tank design and doctrine stagnated.

Tank development in Japan ran contrary to a set of societal norms (what Gerard Hendrik Hofstede would later develop as Cultural Dimensions Theory). While the IJA was strong in the dimension of uncertainty avoidance (which in effect meant that troops rarely deviated from traditional tactics), innovation could still be found. Such innovation came through Japan's realisation that it lagged behind in many aspects of military technology. During the late nineteenth century, Britain had supplied valuable technical assistance in developing modern warships for the Imperial Japanese Navy (IJN). The IJA was also interested in acquiring modern weapons systems, and the European conflagration of 1914–1918 soon gave them ample opportunity to study and later obtain such technology.

During the First World War, Japanese observers noted the astonishingly fast pace at which the principles of armoured warfare developed following the first deployment of British tanks at the Battle of Flers-Courcelette (15–22 September 1916). Forty-nine MK I tanks were made available for the battle, of which thirty-six reached the assembly points. Their subsequent deployment in a breakthrough and exploitation role was only a partial success as no ground of any major strategic value had been captured. Indeed, after the war, Winston Churchill opined that the premature use of tanks to capture 'a few ruined villages' during the third phase of the Somme Offensive had effectively wasted any possibility of a decisive victory in 1916.

The recently published papers of Major Allen Holford-Walker of the Argyll and Sutherland Highlanders largely supports Churchill's view. During the Flers-Courcelette battle, both Major Holford-Walker and his brother Archie (Captain Holford-Walker) were tank commanders. Of the three tanks under Captain Holford-Walker's command, his own tank *Clan Leslie* was rendered *hors de combat* due to damaged axles, the second tank suffered a mechanical failure, while the third ran out of petrol. Of the thirty-six tanks committed to the attack, twenty-seven traversed no man's land to reach the German front line trenches. Having said that, only six tanks penetrated into the German rear areas.

At Flers-Courcelette, the slow-moving tanks were overtaken by the infantry who then found themselves cruelly exposed to German heavy machine gun fire. In the course of the final phase of the Somme Offensive, it was decided that 'the infantry would not wait for the tanks.' In the ensuing Battle of Ancre (13–18 November 1916) inadequate ground analysis led to tanks foundering in the glutinous mud. Once again, the infantry were on their own. Later, Major Holford-Walker wrote that, 'I attribute the fact of the tanks failure to gain their objective to the extraordinary bad ground they had to cross which was worse than I imagined possible.' The failing of the tanks at Ancre and at Arras the following year seemed to confirm the belief that tanks were ineffective weapons of war, and as such 'would have to remain an accessory to a conventional attack, as part of the furniture of tactical attrition.' However, at the Battle of Cambrai (20 November—6 December 1917) the use of tanks *en masse* for the first time proved instrumental in forcing a breach in the German defences. While the gains made were short lived, the spectacular initial gains served to revive the fortunes of this new weapon of war.

Japan's participation in the First World War in alliance with the Entente Powers was largely based on opportunism. German preoccupation with the war in Europe provided favourable circumstances which Japan could exploit in order to expand its sphere of influence in China. Moreover, the conflict between major European industrial powers gave the Japanese the opportunity to study the strategic and tactical transitions that had evolved in the wake of mechanisation and the introduction of ever more sophisticated weapons. The IJA quickly recognised the tank's revolutionary potential and, as early as 1917 had dispatched Captain Mizutani Yoshiho to Great Britain to purchase a Mark IV (Female—armed with machine guns) tank for evaluation. The tank was duly unloaded at the port of Yokohama on 24 October 1918. It was then sent to the infantry school in Chiba Province for testing and evaluation. The following year, six British Whippet tanks and thirteen French Renault FT-17 tanks were also purchased. The newly created Army Technical Headquarters tasked with overseeing weapons research and development stressed the importance of 'employing mechanical power in addition to existing human and animal powers for the operation and transportation of weapons.' This new doctrine generated much interest among more progressive officers who became avid listeners to the lectures on the employment of tanks during the European conflict at Tokyo's Army War College.

While the Whippets were soon regarded as poor investments, the FT-17s went on to form the backbone of the 1st Tank Detachment of the 12th Infantry Division in 1925. This experimental detachment served to create the formulation of the requirements for Japan's first home produced tank. The fledgling tank corps benefited from Minister of War Yamanishi Hanzo's implementation of a modernisation programme which stressed the need for quality over quantity. At the same time, traditionalists clung onto the idea that cavalry still had a part to play in future wars. Despite the unconcealed scorn levelled at them by the traditionalists, the young officers of the tank corps were determined to build a modern armoured force, if necessary from the bottom up.

In the end, the two-stage modernisation programme (August 1922 and April 1923) pleased neither innovators nor traditionalists. The reduction in overall troop numbers by 65,000 was reluctantly accepted by traditionalists as the force structure of twenty-one divisions was kept intact. The innovators wanted even deeper personnel cuts but were satisfied to some extent that a portion of the money saved would be diverted towards tank development. The modernisation programme initially called for the purchase of more foreign tanks. The snag was that neither the British nor the French were prepared to sell their latest models as they were still in the early production stage. The only tanks that were available came from the considerable French holdings of the ageing FT-17. For the Japanese, these obsolete cast-offs represented a dead end in terms of tank design.

General Suzuki (the head of the IJA Technical Bureau) strongly protested against the purchase of any more outdated foreign tanks. His protests were heeded, and soon after the development of the first Japanese tank was placed in the hands of four engineers from the IJA Technical Bureau. One of the officers, the outspoken Tomio Hara clashed repeatedly with the more conservative members of the design team. In spite of this, the Army Staff still agreed to give the designers two years in which to come up with a viable prototype design which could compete with the most modern tanks being manufactured in Europe.

It seemed that Hara and his fellow designers and engineers had been deliberately set an impossible task by the army traditionalists who would have been more than happy to see them fail. Indeed, the odds were stacked against the team as Japan's miniscule automotive industry was based on the production of the entirely hand crafted Mitsubishi Shipbuilding Company Model A sedan (1917–1921) and the small lorries assembled (from American parts) by DAT Jidosha & Co. Ltd. The very limited demand for cars and lorries in Japan simply did not provide the foundations in technical know-how or manufacturing experience for the production of such complex machines as tanks.

To complicate matters even further, the design team were required to work to the strict specifications laid down by the Army Staff. As development of the tank progressed, even more requirements were added. The initial requirements with which Hara and his colleagues began the project are worth noting:

> The total weight should be kept to around twelve tons (not exceeding fifteen tons). The tank should house a crew of five, with a total length of six metres. The dimensions of the tank should not hinder placement on railway transport. The armour should be capable of withstanding an oblique shot by a 37 mm anti-tank gun at a range of 500–600 metres. The tank should have a central rotating turret housing a 57 mm cannon, two machine guns placed in front and rear separate turrets. The engine should have an output of 120 horsepower producing a maximum speed of twenty five kilometres per hour, trench crossing ability of two and a half metres and a climbing radius of forty-three degrees.

The finished design which consisted of more than 10,000 separate elements was submitted for approval in May 1926. Production of the prototype was entrusted to the Osaka Arsenal, although the firms of Mitsubishi and Kawasaki were also subcontracted to fabricate many of the tank's parts. The prototype was completed in February 1927, some two months before the expiry date for the project.

The prototype was manufactured from riveted mild steel as no hardened steel had been made available for the project. In some respects the design resembled a scaled down version of the French Char 2C. Having said that, this was no simple copy as Hara and his team performed minor miracles in getting their own design to the prototype stage. Three months after the completion of the prototype, Experimental Tank No. 1 underwent a road test at the Fuji Exercise Station, followed by cross-country testing at the Tokyo Army Technical Headquarters where it demonstrated a level of mobility and stability which outclassed all current British and French models. During the course of the trials, Hara expressed his sense of satisfaction regarding the tank's performance:

In the eyes of those familiar to us with foreign medium tanks going fourteen kilometres an hour, the appearance of an eighteen ton tank going over twenty kilometres an hour and rushing up the road is spectacular in itself. Adding tank power to our nation's defence I have a sense of trust.

Hara's appraisal of the prototype's performance was soon proved to be hopelessly over-optimistic as the new tank suffered from a number of significant flaws. At eighteen tons, it was both overweight and underpowered in terms of the requirements laid out by the Army Staff. As they could foresee no need for such a cumbersome tank which would clearly be unable to provide direct support to infantry units, Hara and his team were ordered to go back to the drawing board.

Despite the rejection of the prototype by the Army Staff, Hara was pleased with how things were progressing. The trials had clearly demonstrated that Japan possessed the technical know-how and engineering capabilities to build modern tanks. It was his good fortune that shortly after the initial trials had begun, a Vickers Model C tank arrived from Britain. Subsequent comparative tests led to the development of a lighter, faster tank initially known as Experimental Tank No. 2. During the trials of the Vickers Model C, two engineers sent out by the firm were badly burned when petrol fumes seeped inside the tank. Hara later wrote about how the tank engine fire influenced subsequent Japanese tank design:

> The fire in the imported Vickers Model C tank engine was a highly cautionary experience, stressing the fact that fuel with a high flashpoint is desirable since the degree of fire hazard is thus decreased for a tank fighting in a combat environment. Furthermore, since Japan lacks petroleum resources, it was recognised as being more advantageous to use the diesel engine which enjoys less loss in storage/replenishment and less degree of fuel consumption with high thermal efficiency. Thus, from 1932, development on diesel engines was officially initiated.

Official backing for diesel engines meant that the necessary resources for dealing with the engineering problems involved in producing an engine which could cope with the harsh climate in Manchuria would now be made available.

Now brimming with confidence, Hara and his team made rapid progress. In April 1929, the Osaka Army Arsenal completed the construction of the second prototype. Following successful trials and endurance tests it was standardised as the Type 89 medium tank. Production of the Type 89 'A' (fitted with a petrol engine) was assigned to the Sagami Arsenal which subcontracted much of the production work to Mitsubishi Heavy Industries (MHI). As mass production of the Type 89 would take time to set up, several French Renault NC tanks were procured in order to supplement the number of available combat ready tanks in the interim period.

The Renault NC tanks were among the first to see active service with the Japanese tank force when the 1st Special Tank Company went into action with them along with some Type 89s at Harbin during the Manchurian Incident in January 1932. During this operation, the NC tank's poor suspension and the tendency of the engine to overheat generated such a negative impression that it was quickly retired from service. Replacements were not available until the following year when production of the Type 89 began in earnest. In 1936, the Type 89 'B' (fitted with a Mitsubishi air-cooled diesel engine) came into service after years of testing and development. In developing the world's first diesel engine tank, Japan demonstrated that it was a world leader in terms of technical innovation. The battle between innovation and traditionalism was however far from over. After some stunning early operational successes involving the new technology, conservative elements in the Army used their influence to set the clock back to 1918.

1

Innovation and Stagnation
Issues in Japanese Tank Development

The early interwar period produced multifarious hypotheses regarding the employment of tanks on the modern battlefield. That said, opportunities to test these hypotheses were practically non-existent in a world which had shunned military aggression as a means of achieving political goals. The armoured doctrines of the major powers which emerged during this period emphasised the need to mass and concentrate tanks in order to create the necessary conditions for a successful attack. These doctrines also stressed that while the tank was the most important armoured fighting vehicle (AFV), other specialised vehicles would be required to deploy artillery and infantry to the battlefront. Ground analysis and terrain were also significant factors to be taken into consideration as AFVs could only operate in certain conditions. The doctrines which underscored army manuals largely conditioned the design of tanks and other AFVs and their subsequent method of deployment on the battlefield.

Britain had been an early leader in terms of armoured doctrine. The 1929 manual *Mechanised and Armoured Formations* had dealt with combined-arms questions by inferring that in the future, tanks would lead the infantry into the attack. But over the course of the next decade, conservative voices began to reassert themselves, thus ensuring that this valuable doctrinal lead was squandered. Meanwhile, in the Soviet Union, more radical voices were making the case for tanks having a leading role in military operations. In his two seminal doctrinal works *Scale of the Operations of Modern Armies* (1926) and *Characteristics of the Operations of Modern Armies* (1929), General Vladimir Triandafillov expounded his concept of Deep Operations which effectively bridged the gap between strategy and tactics. His methodology called for concentrated forces to attack not just the enemy's first line of contact, but to attack throughout the full depth of the battlefield, destroying the opposition's defensive capabilities and any possibility of reinforcement.

It is uncertain whether Lieutenant-General Yoshikazu Nishi (commanding the Japanese 8th Division in Manchuria) was acquainted with Triandafillov's works. Nonetheless, he was arguably the first tank commander to carry out a deep operation using a combined-arms battle group. Following the conquest of Manchuria and the subsequent establishment of a puppet state (formally recognised by Japan in September 1932), military planners began to look towards consolidating Japan's position by launching Operation Nekka. This operation had two distinct phases, the first involved the capture of the Shanhaiguan Pass at the Great Wall, while the second was concerned with the capture of the province of Rehe which was located on the northern side of the Great Wall. When hopes of persuading the corrupt Fengtian clique warlord and Chairman of the government of Rehe, General Tang Yu-ling to defect to the puppet state failed, the IJA Chief of Staff, Field Marshal Prince Kan'in Kotohito asked the Emperor for permission for the military option to be put into action. The Emperor agreed, with the stipulation that Japanese forces were not to go beyond the Great Wall.

The offensive launched on 23 February 1933 made rapid progress. Within three days the ill prepared and badly equipped Chinese forces had been routed by Nishi's forces at Chaoyang and Kailu. Having suffered a severe mauling, Yu-ling's battered forces retreated towards the provincial capital at Chengde. Nishi resisted the temptation to precipitately don the laurel leaves of victory as he realised that his pursuing infantry lacked the pace to effect a crushing blow before the Chinese set up a new line of defence. While his infantry lacked sufficient speed, the 1st Tank Company which was equipped with eleven Type 89 tanks, two Type 92 heavy armoured cars and approximately 100 trucks was immediately available for the pursuit. Therefore, on 1 March, Nishi ordered Major General Tadashi Kawahara's battle group (an *ad-hoc* combined-arms formation consisting of the 1st Tank Company, a mountain artillery company, an engineer company, two infantry battalions, and a radio communications section) to exploit the initial breakthrough with a drive towards the regional capital.

Kawahara's fast moving column of tanks and trucks raced down the Jinzhou–Chaoyang highway catching Chinese forces who were retreating towards their second line of defences completely off-guard. With his capital about to fall, Yu-ling diverted 200 valuable lorries assigned to his army to transport his accumulated wealth and valuables to Tianjin. Yu-ling's convoy was confiscated *en route* to Chahar by troops loyal to the warlord Zhang Xueliang. Having evaded arrest in Rehe Province, Yu-ling allied himself with the Chahar People's Anti-Japanese Army at Yunzhou. In the meantime, the 1st Tank Company had taken Chengde following a spectacular advance of 320 kilometres in three days. This brilliant breakthrough by mechanised forces against traditional (ill equipped) infantry served to field-test Triandafillov's theory of deep operations and Liddell Hart's theory of combined-arms years before the German Blitzkrieg in the West.

The stunning victory at Rehe provided pro-tank officers like Nishi with the leverage to promote their arguments for the establishment of concentrated armoured formations and combined-arms mechanisation. Their calls were soon answered with the formation of the 1st Independent Mixed Brigade at Kungchuling (Manchuria) in 1934. Japan's first combined-arms formation consisted of two tank battalions, a motorised infantry regiment, and a reconnaissance company. In terms of tank strength, the brigade could field 78 Type 89 tanks and 41 Type 94 tankettes. These medium and light AFVs were well suited to the battlefield conditions encountered. Having said that, the Type 89 was fast becoming obsolete, and consequently the designers went to work on a new medium tank in 1935.

The new medium tank design was inspired to some degree by the British A6 and Medium Mark III tanks. While neither of these models were adopted due to design flaws, their development pointed the way towards a more independent role for tanks in the future. Certainly, the A6, with its 47 mm gun and top speed of fifty kilometres per hour put the Japanese Type 89 tanks at a distinct disadvantage. Reports from the 1st Independent Mixed Brigade in Manchuria indicated that the relatively slow speed (twenty-five kilometres per hour) of the Type 89 meant that it struggled to keep up with faster moving vehicles. As a result, the development by Mitsubishi of a new medium tank and a lighter fast tank was accelerated. Saburo Hyashi, the IJA Chief of Operations was distinctly cool towards the heavier tank design as his estimates were based on peacetime requirements. However, events in China soon changed everything, Hara noting that:

> The equipping of forces with the new tank suddenly developed into a priority problem with the outbreak of the China Incident on 7 July 1937. With this emergency the budget was no longer restricted to a peacetime basis and the formal adoption of the 1st plan was decided unconditionally. In retrospect it may be said that the element of timing was perfect with Chi-Ha tank development.

Accordingly, the decision was made to formally adopt the heavier tank design which was later standardised as the Type 97 Chi-Ha Medium Tank.

The incident referred to by Hara took place at the ancient Marco Polo Bridge located fifteen kilometres south-west of Peking. On the night of 7 July, Japanese infantry on night exercises near Wanping came under fire (the source of this fire has never been determined). The incident sparked off a major war which the IJA High Command had neither anticipated nor planned for. Without the necessary resources to fight a protracted campaign, Japanese military planners quickly developed a strategy which they hoped would force an early Chinese collapse following the encirclement and destruction of their field armies in the north. Confidence in the success of the operation was high, particularly so as the Chinese were contemptuously dismissed as third-class opponents. This early indication of Japanese overconfidence is noteworthy as it was based entirely on spiritual factors rather than sound planning and logistics. The failure to appreciate the importance of logistics would later prove to be Japan's Achilles heel. Edward J. Drea, the noted military historian and expert on the IJA explained the roots of this neglect in his contribution to the book *The Battle for China: Essays on the Military History of the Sino-Japanese War of 1937–1945*:

> The army neglected logistics, with the Staff College favouring instruction in the more glamorous concepts of strategy and tactics rather than the mundane subjects of resupply and maintenance. The infantry scorned men in transport units as second-class troops because many of these fillers had not even completed their basic reserve training and were ineligible for promotion. Promising officer cadets at the military academy ridiculed the supply services, and the army assigned officers who were graduates of the middle schools, not the military academy, to such postings. Officers commanding logistic units were openly regarded as second rate and indeed their designation as special-duty transport troops stamped them as separate and unequal.

The subsequent advance into China ran down two parallel main railway lines—the Tianjin–Pukou route in the east, and the Peking–Wuhan route in the west. These operations imposed huge logistical strains on an army whose administrative margins for supply were always extremely tight.

Inevitably, the attacking Japanese forces overreached themselves. The overexposed IJA 11th Independent Mixed Brigade was counter-attacked by Kuomintang General Tang Enbo's forces at Juyongguan and surrounded. While Chinese forces were also making gains against the Mongolian Army commanded by Prince Teh, the Japanese Chahar Expeditionary Force commanded by Lieutenant-General Hideki Tojo was building up for a major counteroffensive along the Changpei–Kalgan axis. Tojo's forces struck on 18–19 August, quickly taking Shenweitaiko on the Great Wall and the Hanno Dam. The remorseless advance continued, with Kalgan falling to Japanese forces on 27 August.

Following the failure of a counter-attack by General Fu Zuoyi's forces, the Japanese authorities set up the puppet Mongol United Autonomous Government. While on the surface, both Operation Chahar and the subsequent expansion into Shanxi Province had been successful, the 1st Independent Mixed Brigade had not performed particularly well. A post-battle analysis by the Chiba Army Tank School pulled no punches, stating that, 'armoured units were often committed with insufficient preparation, in wet and muddy conditions, without artillery support or coordination.' The failure of the brigade can be attributed almost entirely to Tojo's conservatism which represented the triumph of traditionalism over innovation.

Tojo was a staunch traditionalist who strongly resented the influence of the younger officers who had promoted tank-centred doctrine. As such, he had no intention of allowing tanks to operate independently. The doctrine favoured by Tojo and other traditionalists called for tanks to support the infantry. In their excellent book, *World War II Japanese Tank Tactics*, Gordon L. Rottman and Akira Takizawa outlined the doctrine favoured by traditionalists.

> Typically, a tank regiment would be attached to an infantry division and one of its tank companies to each infantry regiment; the light tank company, if present, was retained for reconnaissance and flank security. When the infantry attacked an enemy position the machine gun was considered the main threat. The artillery was used to suppress the machine guns, but it could not shell enemy positions once the Japanese infantry had approached within 100–150 yards of the objective, for fear of endangering them as they advanced into the open. The infantry employed 7 cm and 7.5 cm battalion guns to cover this range but, being direct-fire weapons, infantry guns were vulnerable to enemy fire and lacked mobility. Other than 5 cm grenade-dischargers, infantry regiments possessed no mortars unless these were attached from non-divisional sources.

Japanese doctrine emphasised the need for the infantry to direct its fire power against enemy anti-tank positions, but a lack of suitable weaponry meant that tanks were frequently used as mobile infantry guns. The use of tanks in this role was strongly opposed by the 1st Independent Mixed Brigade's commander Major-General Koji Sakai. Nonetheless, Tojo broke up the brigade's tank and infantry battalions to reinforce other infantry units. Having seen his brigade stripped to the bone, Sakai cursed his former IJA Academy classmate as a 'stupid moron' whose scepticism and opposition reduced the tank forces into an operational reserve pool to be dispatched to wherever the infantry needed them.

On 7 November 1937, the Japanese formed the Central China Field Army. The Japanese commanders on the ground favoured a rapid advance to Nanjing, believing it to be a golden opportunity to comprehensively defeat the Chinese, and thus bring the war to a successful conclusion. The Chinese Nationalist leader Chiang Kai-shek vacillated, writing on 17 November, 'Should we defend Nanjing or abandon it? It is hard to decide.' Two days later, having reached a decision, he appointed Tang Shengzhi as commander of the Nanjing garrison. On paper at least, Tang's forces appeared formidable. At his disposal he had thirteen divisions, three of which had been trained by German instructors. Moreover, he had approximately fifteen German Panzer I Ausf. A tanks available for the defence.

But in reality his forces were weak, with the bulk of his exhausted and demoralised troops having recently experienced the fall of Shanghai. The German tanks at his disposal were also ill-suited to China's climate and terrain and would therefore be of little use in the coming battle. Chiang was well aware of the shortcomings of his forces, and following a tour of inspection of Nanjing's defences on 27 November wrote, 'It is hard to defend Nanjing, but we must do it.'

On 10 December, Japanese engineers were successful in creating a breach in the Guanghua Gate in the east of the city. Fierce fighting followed in which some of the Chinese Panzer I's attempted to halt the Japanese advance. The situation was however hopeless, and bowing to the inevitable, Chiang issued orders for Tang to 'retreat when the conditions are untenable.' By the evening of 12 December, the retreat had turned into a rout. The remaining Panzer I's were abandoned by the riverside in the southern Xiaguan District as they could not be ferried to safety. Some of these tanks were later displayed in Tokyo, but for political reasons were described as having been produced in the Soviet Union.

Japanese successes in China created an aura of invincibility. In reality they had served to conceal some serious shortcomings within the Army. In 1937, logistical problems impacted upon operations in north China and Shanghai due to the inability of Japan's limited industrial base to maintain adequate levels of supply. Unexpectedly heavy Chinese resistance also served to slow down the advance as Japanese commanders frequently resorted to dated and unimaginative tactics which proved to be very costly in terms of time and men. Chinese losses may have been heavier, but the creaking Nationalists somehow managed to fight on, denying the Japanese outright victory. With neither side able to comprehensively defeat the other, a stalemate developed. To bring this increasingly costly war to a satisfactory conclusion, Japan needed to employ new tactics.

In May 1938, the success of the Iwanka Detachment and the Imada Detachment at the Battle of Hsuchou seemed to point the way towards the employment of more progressive tactics. During the course of the operation, these fast motorised detachments consisting of a tank battalion supported by infantry, artillery and engineer units prevented Chinese forces from retreating from Hsuchou by cutting rail communications to Chengchou. Following the demolition of the bridge at Handaokouji, the Japanese detachments returned to their own lines having only suffered light casualties.

The successful attack received maximum publicity in the Japanese press. Notwithstanding, conservative elements within the Army remained highly sceptical about the effectiveness of independent tank formations. Consequently, few Army commanders gained any real understanding about the capabilities and limitations of modern armoured forces. Their lack of foresight would have disastrous consequences the following year when tensions with the Soviets along the Halka River culminated in the so-called Nomonhan Incident.

2

A Mauling by the Red Bear
Japanese Tank Deficiencies are Laid Bare during the Undeclared Border Conflicts with the Soviet Union

The 1909 IJA field manual emphasised the need to instil spiritual factors into the troops. These factors included the individual soldier's unshakable belief in his cause, a tenacious and aggressive attitude born out of love of country, and the belief that Japan's destiny was to forge a great empire. It was believed that such abstractions would compensate for Japan's deficiencies in technology and material. In 1939, the IJA was still largely an infantry force whose more recent combat experience had been in fighting against Chinese warlord and nationalist armies that possessed few tanks and had minimal anti-tank capability. Japanese doctrine appeared to have been vindicated in China, as time and time again, numerically inferior forces had succeeded in routing much larger Chinese units. In planning for war against the Soviet Union, the IJA still believed that spiritual factors would suffice to overcome the superior firepower of the Red Army's infantry, artillery and tank forces. When the infantry heavy Japanese forces clashed with Soviet mechanised units at Nomonhan in May 1939, the IJA's faith in abstract factors would be cruelly disabused.

Between 1934 and 1938, Soviet military capability along the vast state's eastern border was hugely improved by better rail communications, the construction of fortifications, and significant reinforcements of both troops and heavy weaponry. Predictably, tensions along the border were heightened, and 'incidents and provocations' with the Japanese Kwantung Army became an almost daily occurrence. By the end of June 1937, it was estimated that there had been no fewer than 185 border incidents. With no relaxing of tensions, it was inevitable that a serious border conflict between Soviet and Japanese forces would erupt sooner or later.

In July 1938, a 'divisional-scale conflict' broke out on an area of elevated ground known as the Changkufeng Heights lying to the south-west of Lake

Khasan. At this point where Manchuria, Korea and the Soviet Union all meet, a bitter border conflict was fought as Red Army forces attempted to hold back a Japanese advance involving infantry, cavalry and artillery which threatened the Soviet naval base at Vladivostok. The Soviet response was swift, their fierce counter-attack utilising 257 T-26 tanks, eighty one BT-7 light tanks and thirteen SU-5-2 self-propelled guns dislodged the Japanese from their newly won positions on the heights. The heavily outnumbered Japanese battalions fought bravely, and were able to inflict heavy losses on the Soviet forces.

In Tokyo the incident was seen as something of an embarrassment as Japanese units had been forced back to their starting points. Misplaced faith in the value of martial spirit in overcoming the modern machinery of war contributed to the high Japanese casualties incurred during the fighting. As no Japanese armoured formations took part in this clash, the IJA were not able to take any lessons on board with regard to any future confrontations involving armour. Consequently, the belief persisted that Japanese tanks were more than adequate to defeat the Soviets in the inevitable major clash of arms hotly anticipated by army commanders.

In May 1939, heavy fighting between Japanese and Soviet forces erupted near Nomonhan, a small village located on the ill-defined Manchurian–Outer Mongolian border. Japanese rules of engagement stipulated that an incursion by Outer Mongolian troops across the Halha River had to be met by overwhelming force. On 21 May, the 64th Regiment of the 23rd Infantry Division commanded by Colonel Yamagata Takemitsu attempted to trap the intruders between Nomonhan and the Khalkin River. Takemitsu's combativeness was bolstered by the firm belief that only the second-rate Soviet troops of the 7th Border Guard Brigade would be available to support the Outer Mongolian forces. IJA planners had based their estimates on established doctrine which held that major military operations could not be conducted more than 200–250 kilometres from a railhead. The lack of understanding demonstrated by the IJA would soon contribute to a disaster as the high command simply could not recognise that their fossilised thinking was not keeping pace with current developments.

On 28 May, a detachment led by Lieutenant-Colonel Yaozo Azuma attempted to block the Kawamata Bridge in order to trap retreating enemy troops. Instead of trapping lightly armed border troops, Azuma's detachment soon found itself encircled by regular Soviet tank and motorised units. The skilfully executed trap sprung by combined Soviet tank-infantry units holding the high ground succeeded in destroying more than sixty per cent of Azuma's unit. While the severity of the fighting caught the Japanese off guard, they recovered quickly. In late June, the Kwantung Army headquarters decided to commit two task forces including the 3rd and 4th Tank Regiments to a decisive battle 'to expel the invaders.' On 2 July, Japanese forces scored some early successes by taking Hill 721 and forcing a crossing of the Halha River. The task of driving Soviet troops from the east bank of the Halha was entrusted to Lieutenant-General Masaomi Yasuoka who decided to commit his tanks to a night attack designed to break through the Soviet lines and advance towards the Kawamata Bridge. Yasuoka's tactics turned out to be as flawed as the high command's outdated doctrines. Believing Soviet troops to be dull-witted and lacking initiative, he sacrificed planning for speed, hoping to trap an enemy whose fighting capabilities he greatly underestimated.

There is an old saying, 'Fail to prepare, prepare to fail'— the pervasiveness of excessive Japanese pride was such that Yasuoka did not even consider the possibility of failure. As a result his haste ensured that in the coming battle there was no coordination among his infantry, artillery, and tank forces. Japanese armoured doctrine stressed that in pursuit operations tanks were to be employed to chase the retreating enemy, and in doing so, deny them any possibility of reforming. The Military Intelligence Division of the U.S. Army Special Series (No. 34) manual provides the best outline of Japanese pursuit doctrine:

> The Japanese feel that pursuit affords the best opportunity for exploiting the advantages of the tanks to the maximum... Clear objectives are selected, and the tanks are ordered to proceed against them as directly as possible regardless of losses. Pursuit, the Japanese say, should be unremitting and audacious, even if only one tank survives to complete the mission.

Yasuoka's pursuit operation required a little more thought as Soviet artillery on the Halha's west bank meant that his tanks would be presented as easy targets as they advanced down the basin-like slopes which led to the east bank of the river. Knowing that a daylight attack would most likely result in significant losses for no appreciable gain, Yasuoka opted for a night attack. This decision created problems of its own as the tank crews were simply not equipped for night operations, nor were they fully appraised of the enemy's strength or dispositions.

Unsurprisingly, the attack turned into a somewhat chaotic affair as driving rain further impeded Japanese coordination. Nonetheless, it appeared that the Soviet troops were on the run. As night turned to day, Japanese forces seemed to be making progress, encountering weak opposition from Soviet troops who appeared to be living up to the stereotypes by which they were characterised. Appearances can however be deceptive, and over the next few days of fierce fighting, Soviet resistance stiffened. The Red Army's multi-layered defence system meant that a Japanese breakthrough at any point could not be fully exploited as pre-registered artillery could drench the area in shellfire. As more

Soviet reinforcements arrived, the Japanese commanders faced a race against time as their own fragile logistical tail could not cope with the strains of protracted combat.

In four days of fighting, the Japanese lost forty-two of the seventy-three tanks committed to the attack. The majority of the lightly armoured Japanese Type 89, Type 97, Type 95, Type 94 tanks, and Type 97 tankettes were destroyed by Soviet 45 mm tank and anti-tank guns which had better range and penetrating power than the weaker guns installed in Yasuoka's tanks. While a significant number of Japanese tanks were later recovered, the experience of combat against a more technologically sophisticated enemy was a chastening one.

Having failed to score a rapid and decisive victory, the Japanese forces were now locked into a war of attrition which they were forced to fight in a doctrinal vacuum. One Japanese misconception about Soviet capabilities led to another. While all offensives are subject to the law of diminishing returns, it was thought that the Red Army could not sustain any offensive operations long enough to achieve worthwhile results. Therefore, few Japanese troops bothered to dig proper shelters as they thought that they would be soon vacating them once they had resumed their own offensive.

The stalling of the Japanese offensive presented opportunities for a creative counterblow by Soviet forces. Soviet Corps Commander Georgy Zhukov quickly formulated a plan to encircle Japanese forces within the disputed border area. Following Stalin's acceptance of the plan, he was given overall command of Soviet forces, effectively replacing Army Commander 1st Grade G. M. Shtern who was technically his superior. Zhukov asked for and received additional forces consisting of aircraft, a tank brigade, artillery, and three rifle divisions. On 15 July, the reinforced 57th Special Corps was redesignated as the 1st Army Group.

Zhukov now had more than adequate forces at his disposal, but supply remained a problem as his proposed operation would take place some 650 kilometres from the nearest railhead. To ensure a steady flow of supplies, motor transport of all type was pressed into service, Zhukov later noting that, 'This effort dwarfed the logistical preparations of the Japanese; indeed, it dwarfed anything the Japanese believed possible.' Japanese officers did indeed think that such a logistical operation was way beyond the capability of any army. Although it has to be said that not everyone was fooled, particularly those ordinary soldiers who had the unenviable job of occupying the forward positions. They may not have understood logistic complexities, but they still sensed that something was afoot.

Effective Soviet deception measures (*maskirovka*) ensured that when the attack was launched, complete tactical surprise would be achieved. In his memoirs, Marshal Zhukov recalled some of the methods employed:

The concentration of forces—of shock groups on the flanks—and the movement of troops to the jumping-off areas had to occur in the small hours of 20 August. By dawn everything was to be concealed in the thick brush along the river in specially prepared shelters. Pieces of ordinance, mortars, vehicles and all other equipment were hidden under camouflage nets made of material that we found available on the spot. The tank units were moved to the jumping-off areas in small groups from different directions shortly before the artillery attack and air raids ...

During the night all movements were 'jammed' by noise specially created by aircraft, artillery, mortar, machine-gun and rifle fire, conducted according to a strict schedule that was dovetailed with the movements.

For purposes of camouflage, we used special sound equipment which imitated aircraft engines, the movement of tanks, the driving in of wooden piles, etc. We began to use this equipment 12–15 days before the planned movement of the shock groups to accustom the Japanese to these noises. At the beginning the Japanese mistook them for real troop movements and began to fire at the areas from which the noises came. Later, they either got used to it or realised what it was, and usually stopped paying attention to all noises, which was exactly what we wanted during the real regrouping and concentration of forces.

At 06.30 hrs on 20 August, Zhukov launched his offensive by sending in bombers and fighter aircraft to bomb and strafe Japanese artillery positions. A near total failure of Japanese intelligence gathering and interpretation meant that the build-up of three Soviet rifle divisions and seven armoured brigades largely went unnoticed. Zhukov had achieved what he wanted, complete tactical surprise.

Throughout the day, a series of Soviet probes succeeded in fixing the Japanese forces in place for the tanks to encircle and destroy. With more than 500 tanks and 400 armoured cars at his disposal, Zhukov was in a position to execute a Soviet blitzkrieg in the form of a double-envelopment. In his memoirs, Zhukov described how the offensive unfolded:

At nine sharp, when our aircraft were strafing the enemy and bombing his artillery, red flares went up announcing the beginning of the offensive. The attacking units, covered by artillery fire, charged.

Our air and artillery strike was so powerful and successful that the enemy was morally and physically depressed. During the first hour and a half he could not even return the gun fire. The Japanese observation posts, communication lines, and fire positions were destroyed ...

Desperate fighting went on during 21–22 August, especially in the area of Bolshiye Peski, where the enemy offered more obstinate resistance than we thought he would. To rectify the miscalculation we had to bring in the 9th Armoured Brigade from the reserve and reinforce our artillery.

After destroying the flanking groups of the enemy, our armoured and motorised units closed the circle around the 6th Japanese Army by the evening of 26 August and thereupon began to split and destroy the surrounded enemy ...

The Japanese fought to the last man. But gradually their soldiers came to realise the flimsiness of the official propaganda that the Imperial Army was invincible, since it was suffering incredibly heavy casualties without winning a single battle for four months.

This classic Soviet battle of encirclement involved the establishment of an outer line of defence to ward off Japanese relief attempts, while an inner front concentrated on destroying the encircled enemy. Thus, it can be said that Zhukov imposed the Soviet way of war upon a Japanese foe whose doctrine meant that officers were simply unable to adapt to the demands of fighting a defensive battle.

Japanese losses at Nomonhan were staggering, with an overall casualty rate of seventy-three per cent. Although, these numbers may have been inflated by the Japanese authorities who listed troops who had surrendered as having been killed in action. There were certainly lessons to be learned from the disaster, but instead of reflecting, the IJA high command disciplined some troops while lauding others as heroes. Some officers who had survived the battle were branded as cowards and were even pressured into committing suicide. Senior commanders and staff officers were effectively demoted by being transferred to reserve units or training schools. The meaning of these punishments was clear; the only path was victory or death. More than anyone, the actions of First-Lieutenant Tetsuo Sadakaji exemplified the kind of Japanese spirit (*Yamatodamushi*) demanded by the High Command. The battalion war diary described his actions:

First Lieutenant Sadakaji swinging his sword over his head, led several members of his machine-gun company in a desperate counter-attack on the tanks. Their ability to damage the enemy tanks was nil, but the attack probably panicked the tank crews who abruptly retreated. The tanks were probably part of a probe for artillery survey and registration as well as armed reconnaissance of our positions.

On the surface, the actions of this officer may appear as merely foolhardy or suicidally brave. Delving deeper, it can be argued that they characterised 'the dilemma of doctrine and force structure which impaled the Japanese.' The numerous army investigatory committees which looked into the causes of the disaster concluded that fighting spirit remained at the heart of modern warfare, although it was conceded that spiritual power would in the future need to be augmented by more firepower in the form of effective anti-tank weapons.

The tank losses incurred at Nomonhan, particularly those during the fighting near the Halka River clearly demonstrated the urgent need to upgrade the anti-tank capability of the Type 97 tank, whose short-barrelled 57 mm gun lacked penetrating power. Subsequently, the Type 1 47 mm anti-tank gun was designed to counter the effective 45 mm gun mounted in the Soviet BT-7 tank. Testing of the 'Experimental Type 97 47 mm anti-tank gun' took place between 1938 and 1939. The prototype was not accepted for service as it was deemed to lack sufficient armour penetrating power. An improved version was quickly developed, and following approval went into production at the Osaka Arsenal in 1941. The following year, a variant of this gun was installed in the Type 97 tank following modifications to the hull and turret. These modifications were fairly simple as the original fighting compartment design included additional space which to some extent future-proofed the tank. The improved design was redesignated as the Type 97 *Kai Shinhoto Chi-Ha*. Mass production of this new model began in 1942. During the same period, three-hundred older Type 97 tanks were modified to accept the new gun.

The Type 97 47 mm anti-tank gun was the first truly indigenous weapon of its type to be produced in Japan. Arguably, the main reason why it was accepted was not its performance, but rather that the ammunition it used was the same as the regular ground forces. By early-to-mid-war standards, its performance was adequate. However, lessons learned from the fighting in Europe made it clear that the requirement for larger calibre guns was becoming a priority. By the time the improved Type 97 entered the combat arena it was already outclassed by the latest Allied tanks. During the fighting in China and Manchuria, neither the armament nor the armour protection on Japanese tanks had been tested against armour with similar characteristics. As a consequence, the development of new tanks to face the technologically superior Allied armour was problematical. Searching for inspiration, Japanese designers turned to its most technologically advanced Tripartite partner.

3

'Don't Miss the Bus'
Stalemate in China and the Employment of Japanese Tanks during the Expansion of the War into South-East Asia

Encouraged by the Japanese reversal at Nomonhan, Chinese Nationalist forces launched a nationwide offensive employing seventy divisions in mid-December 1939. Lieutenant-General Yasuji Okamura's 11th Army found itself hard pressed defending frontages as long as 160 kilometres. In spite of this, the Chinese offensive never gained momentum due to diversions caused by escalating tensions with Mao's Communists. By mid-January 1940, Japanese forces had regrouped and were able to launch a series of counter-attacks which brought Chiang's forces to a halt within four weeks. The series of hard-fought battles in southern China succeeded in driving the Chinese Nationalist forces back to their bases and restoring Japanese zones of control. Notwithstanding the ultimate failure of Chiang's offensive, the fact that he was able to muster the necessary forces to launch it made it abundantly clear to the Japanese High Command that the war in China was far from over.

The prospect of an endless war in China was one that the Japanese General Staff and the War Ministry could not accept. In March 1940, both the staff and the ministry concluded that the war in China needed to be brought to an end by the end of the year. In the meantime, the Japanese China Expeditionary Army would effectively need to become self-sufficient as the four-year plan for rearming and modernising the Imperial land forces for the anticipated war against the Soviet Union had priority. Then, like a sudden bolt from the blue, Hitler's Blitzkrieg against France and the Low Countries in May–June 1940 changed everything. The Japanese military leadership were so intoxicated by Hitler's seemingly easy victories that they quickly forgot their gloomy predictions about a stalemated war in China. That was not all, as they also strongly advocated taking advantage of Britain's weak position by launching an immediate attack on Singapore. Conservatives within the Japanese cabinet may have been successful in suppressing this scheme, but they failed to eradicate the spirit of opportunism which not only lingered, but continued to grow as the lure of oil and other precious raw materials in South-East Asia proved irresistible.

By mid-1940, the militarists had all but convinced Prime Minister Fumimaro Konoe and his cabinet that military expansion into South-East Asia was absolutely necessary for national survival. Their 'Don't miss the bus' policy was wholly opportunistic and lacking in political and strategic insight. For the militarists, the abundant raw resources in French Indochina were, 'a treasure lying in the street just waiting to be picked up.' On 22 September 1940, Japanese troops entered the resource rich territory. Too weak to resist militarily, the Vichy French authorities reluctantly agreed to the occupation of northern Indochina. This naked aggression drew protests from Foreign Minister Yosuke Matsuoka and the more reflective members of the High Command who foresaw the inevitability of war with the democratic powers.

On 28 September 1940, America responded to Japanese aggression and their entry into the Tripartite Pact with Germany and Italy by placing an embargo on scrap iron and steel shipments to Japan. Britain, now free from the threat of German invasion also acted by abandoning its policy of appeasing Japan by reopening the Burma Road and supporting China with a loan of £10,000,000. British support for China added a sense of urgency to Japanese operations which entered a new phase in November 1940 with a limited offensive that had the aim of relieving the threat of a flanking attack by Mao's Communist forces in the area between Ching-men and Ta-hung Shan. On 25 November, several Japanese columns began the opening phase of the Han River Operation with advances towards Hengtien and Yen-chih-miao. Meanwhile, the Kitano Force (comprised of elements of the 4th Division and the 7th and 13th Tank Regiments) had forged ahead with a drive aimed at deep penetration into the Chinese positions at Liang-shui-ching, Hsia-chia-tzu, and Kuai-huo-pu. Two columns of the Kitano Force faced hard fighting the following day as they came up against determined resistance at Li-chia-tang.

The blunting of the Japanese advance provided the opportunity for an effective counterstroke. At dusk on 27 November, elements of the 27th, 31st and 44th Divisions of the National Revolutionary Army (NRA) launched attacks in several locations. Crumbling under the hammer blows of the relentless Chinese assaults, Japanese troops began to fall back. Bowing to the inevitable, Lieutenant-General Waichiro Sonobe issued orders on the following day for his troops to withdraw to their original positions. The withdrawal almost turned into a disaster as the retreating troops were harried west of the Xiang River. Japanese casualties were heavy, but would have been yet heavier still if it had not been for the timely arrival of tanks and aircraft which provided effective cover.

Japanese armoured doctrine almost exclusively emphasised offensive operations. As a consequence the defence was downgraded to a 'temporary phase of combat' which had to be accepted because of overwhelming enemy superiority. Even when such circumstances arose, Japanese commanders could not bring themselves to talk about retreats and withdrawals. Instead, they issued orders for 'advances to a strategic location' A characteristic of these 'advances' was the sacrificing of rear-guard units whose suicidal defence would buy time for the main body of troops to withdraw. At the Xiang River, the intelligent use of Japanese armour meant that troops who would normally have been sacrificed by costly *Banzai* tactics lived to fight another day.

While military stalemate ensued in China, the Japanese could at least claim a major success on the diplomatic front. On 13 April 1941, Stalin's toast of '*Banzai* for His Majesty the Emperor' sealed the neutrality pact with Japan at a lavish ceremony in the Kremlin. For Matsuoka, the pact meant that there was now, 'nothing to fear in the whole world.' Three months later, Japan's Basic National Guidelines which focused on the total occupation of French Indochina were ratified by the Emperor. On 24 July 1941, Japanese forces moved in to occupy the remainder of the Vichy French territories. America responded swiftly with an intensification of economic sanctions which included the freezing of Japanese assets and credits. This action was followed by a total embargo on all oil products. The British and Dutch followed with their own economic counter-measures. In Tokyo, the High Command was faced with a dilemma regarding operations in China which were already proving to be a severe strain on Japan's limited resources. The cutting off of precious oil supplies left Japan with little room for manoeuvre. The choice was a simple one, either the nation accepted the terms dictated by Washington, or they prepared for war.

On 16 October 1941, Konoe and his entire cabinet resigned. That same day, General Tojo received the royal mandate. Any influence the moderates had was now lost as Japan was inexorably set upon a major confrontation with America and Britain. A meeting of the Supreme War Council on 4 November produced an optimistic assessment of Japan's chances of defeating the western democracies in a short but decisive contest. At an Imperial Conference held on the following day, the Emperor stated that Japan should go to war if negotiations in Washington were not completed by 1 December. Later this deadline was extended to 8 December in order to give Japanese diplomats more time to play out their elaborate charade in Washington.

With talks effectively deadlocked over the intractable question of Japanese involvement in China and French Indochina, the Imperial War Council in Tokyo decided that diplomacy had served its purpose. Long before Washington's response to Japan's latest diplomatic proposals was known, a mobile task force of six aircraft carriers, two battle cruisers and nine destroyers had already began stealthily steaming towards the American naval base at Pearl Harbour. The Japanese plan known as Operation Z was bold and did not wholly anticipate the element of tactical surprise. The attack was still underway on the morning of 7 December when a hastily convened war conference was held at the White House in Washington. The meeting was constantly interrupted by messages coming from Pearl Harbour and overseas territories under attack. One caller was the British Prime Minister Winston Churchill who enquired, 'Mr President, what's all this about Japan?' Having been appraised of the situation, Churchill reported that Malaya was also under attack.

Meanwhile in the Philippines, General Douglas MacArthur had been recalled to duty following his retirement four years earlier. Neither he nor the Chiefs of Staff in Washington expected the Japanese to attack before the spring of 1942. Little did they know that the Japanese were working to their own time-table. Within hours of the attack on Pearl Harbour, a Japanese amphibious assault force was menacing the Philippine coast. Hampered by the unworkable Rainbow-5 defence plan, MacArthur's command was in these first few hours of crisis characterised by confusion and indecision.

The Japanese took full advantage of the situation, and by 10 December had landed 43,000 troops on Luzon. On 22 December, the first tank-versus-tank engagement of the Pacific War took place when Lieutenant-Colonel Shoji Kumagaya's Type 95 Ha-Go tanks ambushed a patrol consisting of M3 Stuart tanks from the American 192nd Tank Battalion near Damortis. By 26 December, Japanese forces concentrated at two points to break through the heavily defended Agno River line. Intense infantry and tank fire repulsed the first Japanese attack, but any prolonged defence would be hindered by a lack of high explosive rounds. Heavy Japanese artillery and mortar counter-fire eventually subdued the defenders. Japanese troops were then able to secure a lodgement to the east of Carmen, forcing the 26th Philippine Cavalry to withdraw. More Japanese troops then poured into the gap. Soon, the whole east flank had collapsed, precipitating the hasty retreat of American and Philippine troops to the next defence line which ran from the mountains west of Santa Ignacia to the mountains east of San Jose.

On 26 December, MacArthur declared Manila an open city. Lieutenant-General Masaharu Homma commanding Japanese forces on Luzon realised that the decisive battle would now be fought on Bataan. The occupation and administration of Manila would cost Homma precious troops, and above all, time. Therefore, in order to maintain the impetus of his attack, he dispatched Colonel Seinosuke Sonada's 7th Tank Regiment to strike out towards the important road junction at Plaridel and the Calumput bridges along Route 5. On the morning of 31 December, Sonada's tanks reached the outskirts of Baliuag. The bridge across the stream had been blown, and while engineers repaired the damage, the tank crews waited. In carefully concealed positions, a platoon of M3 Stuarts from the 192nd Tank Battalion waited for the moment to pour fire on the unsuspecting Japanese. It must have been a moment of sweet revenge for the American tankers who had themselves been ambushed nine days earlier. Their ambush slowed down the Japanese advance by several hours, and it was not until the early afternoon that Japanese units were able to penetrate the eastern outskirts of the town.

These small victories did little to impede the relentless Japanese advance. Without an effective defensive strategy, MacArthur's forces were forced back to the Bataan Peninsula. On the orders of the President, a reluctant MacArthur was evacuated to Australia on 11 March 1942. Meanwhile the situation on Bataan became increasingly desperate with disease rampant and food supplies only sufficient for a diet consisting of 1,000 calories per day. On 3 April, the Japanese attacked the weakened defenders who somehow managed to hold out for five days. General Jonathan Wainwright pulled back to the Corregidor fortress from where he intended to make a last stand. Corregidor was indeed a tough nut to crack, as its numerous coastal defence batteries pointed menacingly out to sea. Any Japanese landing force would also have to contend with the extensive tunnels and galleries which connected scores of bunkers and concrete emplacements.

Following the fall of Bataan, the Japanese put much thought into the conquest of the Corregidor fortress. A crack unit including elements from the 7th Tank Regiment was formed to support the landings. Early skirmishes with American M3 Stuart tanks on Luzon had clearly demonstrated the shortcomings of the main armament mounted on the Type 97 Chi-Ha tank. The short-barrelled 57 mm gun was incapable of penetrating enemy armour except at close range. In order to gain some advantage, a handful of the new Shinhoto Chi-Ha tanks mounting the more effective high-velocity 47 mm gun was delivered in time for the assault.

The fortress was softened up by waves of bombers and artillery fire from Japanese emplacements on the tip of the Bataan Peninsula. The assault preparations intensified on 4 May, when over 16,000 shells smashed into the island. The landing, carried out on the following day, met fierce initial opposition. The turning point came when Japanese troops succeeded in forming a small bridgehead into which they brought ashore two Shinhoto Chi-Ha tanks and a captured American M3 Stuart which was commanded by the detachment leader Major Matsuoka. The sudden appearance of Matsuoka's tanks near the main tunnel complex helped to make Wainwright realise the hopelessness of his position. In order to avoid total slaughter, the American commander surrendered the island and its 11,000 defenders. Little did he know that Homma's forces were themselves close to the point of exhaustion. Homma had gambled and won. The ace up his sleeve were the tanks of the Matsuoka detachment which he used skilfully and imaginatively. Indeed, throughout the campaign in the Philippines, Japanese tanks had played an important part in maintaining the pace of the advance, harassing the retreating enemy, and exploiting weak points in the hastily manned joint American–Philippine defence lines.

The successful expansionist drive into South-East Asia saw the fruits of victory tumbling into Japanese hands even more quickly than they had anticipated. Consequently, China's importance as a theatre of war diminished. Lacking sufficient troops, weapons and equipment, the operations of Japanese forces were largely limited to 'pre-empting Chinese counter-offensives or nipping them in the bud.' Limited offensives were carried out, but they were based upon holding the major cities and rail communications in 'point and line' tactics dictated by the unfavourable force to space ratio. Plans to concentrate sixteen divisions in south-central China for a decisive assault on Chiang's forces in Sichuan province came to nothing as changing strategic priorities drew away troops and resources. Armoured units withdrawn from China included the 6th and 14th Tank Regiments, which along with the 1st tank Regiment from the homeland formed the 3rd Tank Group which was subordinated to the 25th Army that was to invade Malaya. The 7th Tank Regiment was withdrawn at the same time and attached to the 14th Army for the planned invasion of the Philippines. At around the same time, the 8th and 9th Tank Regiments were sent to reinforce the Kwantung Army in Manchuria.

Taking advantage of the respite, Chinese forces reorganised. Increased assistance from the Allies also enabled Chiang to partially redress the balance of forces. With the transfer of a substantial number of tanks from China, subsequent engagements at Changsha, Zhejiang-Jiangxi, West-Hubei and Changde were fought largely with infantry. Dogged Chinese resistance meant that Japanese forces were unable to deal the long hoped for knock-out blow. The long period of stalemate which ensued was not to be broken until the launching of the Japanese *Ichi-Go* operation in April 1944. In the meantime, the semi-autonomous Kwantung Army continued to direct its unwavering gaze towards the Soviet Union. The neutrality pact with Stalin served to provide breathing space in which the reorganisation of Japanese forces in Manchuria could be completed before the inevitable clash of arms. Two tank divisions were formed in Manchuria during 1942. Having said that, overall numbers of tanks remained much the same as no new tank regiments were formed due to a fall in tank production after the wartime peak was reached in early 1942. Limited new production resulted in an increasingly obsolete armoured force. Yet despite this, Japanese tanks went on to achieve spectacular successes in Malaya and the Philippines where a winning combination of tanks and bombers would bring the Allies to their knees.

4

Bicycles and Tank Tracks
The Impact of Japanese tanks on the Malayan Campaign

The invasion of Malaya and the subsequent drive towards Singapore arguably represented the apogee of Japanese armoured operations during the Second World War. The assault began on 8 December 1941 with a shore bombardment which was followed by a landing of the crack Japanese 18th Infantry Division at Kota Bharu on Malaya's north-east coast. Meanwhile, the 5th Infantry Division pre-empted British defensive plans by swiftly occupying Pattani and Songkhla on Thailand's east coast. Having been forestalled by the Japanese, British Commonwealth forces occupied the fortified Jitra position located near the west coast of Malaya, close to the Thai border. The Japanese forces had only scanty information available about the Jitra position, meaning that their advance would entail some degree of risk. To offset this risk, the Saeki Detachment formed around the 3rd Company of the 1st Tank Regiment was available to exploit any vulnerabilities in the British defences.

Lieutenant-Colonel Shizuo Saeki's small force consisted of two companies of Ha-Go light tanks, one company of Chi-Ha medium tanks, two companies of motorised infantry, one platoon of engineers, a medical section, and a signals section. The detachment was specifically tasked with achieving a breakthrough on the Singora Road, located south of the river valley. Everything depended on rapid manoeuvre, a prerequisite for success which was not lost on Lieutenant Yamane who commanded the armoured spearhead. Prior to the operation he was heard to state emphatically that, 'If one vehicle becomes immobile, abandon it and continue the advance. If two vehicles are immobilised, abandon them and advance. Run over enemy or even friends and advance until immobilised.'

On the afternoon of 11 December, the Japanese attack spearheaded by the Saeki Detachment crashed into the Indian troops manning the British defensive line. Having never encountered tanks before, panic set in amongst the Indian troops. Major-General Murray-Lyon commanding the British Commonwealth forces requested permission to fall back to a more defensible position within the natural stronghold of Gurun located just under fifty kilometres south of Jitra. General Arthur Percival in overall command of British Commonwealth forces in Malaya refused because of the deleterious effect on moral such an early withdrawal would produce. As Percival saw it, there was no other alternative to holding the line at Jitra.

During the course of the Japanese advance, tanks were always at the front. Tank guns proved very effective at both blasting a path through defensive positions and forcing the enemy troops to keep their heads down. At Jitra, Japanese tanks employed in non-standard ways were effective combat multipliers, their mobility and firepower being used to fix the enemy in position while supporting infantry turned the flanks. With his forces effectively scattered by the relentless Japanese advance, Murray-Lyon was finally given permission to withdraw to the fall-back position at Gurun. Executed far too late, the withdrawal was characterised by chaotic scenes as communications had all but broken down. Taking advantage of the situation, Japanese tanks and infantry entered the undefended streets of Jitra. Their relentless advance then continued with the capture of the airfield at Alor Star, where 'they found porridge still warm in the RAF officer's mess.' An attempt to take the bridge over the River Bata by storm fared less well as it was repulsed by elements of the Gurkha Rifles. This setback proved to be a temporary one, as by the following day, Japanese units led by tanks were once again heading south. Lacking supplies, they seized undamaged supply dumps and abandoned vehicles which served both to sustain and speed up their advance towards Singapore.

The Japanese tanks employed during the fighting for the Jitra position succeeded for a number of reasons. First, Lieutenant-Colonel Saeki demonstrated a willingness to take risks. Second, the Indian units sent to Malaya had never encountered tanks before. Third, the British and Indian units had lost many of their radios, and as a result, they were unable to coordinate their defence. Fourth, the rapid pace of the Japanese advance meant that the defending forces were always in a reactive rather than a proactive position. Fifth, and arguably most significantly, the British opinion at the time was that tanks were unsuitable for jungle warfare. The Japanese Type 97 medium tanks employed at Jitra would have been highly vulnerable to the British 2-Pounder gun mounted on the Matilda and Valentine tank. Unfortunately for the British command, none were available. A lack of armour and sufficient anti-tank weaponry had even more disastrous consequences as the retreat from northern Malaya was turned into a rout by rampaging Japanese tank formations.

In the early hours of 7 January 1942, Japanese troops overran the British Commonwealth defensive positions at Trolak, eight kilometres north of the Slim River. Caught completely off guard by the collapse at Trolak, the defenders of the vital road bridge at Slim River were unable to stop the advance of Major Toyusaku Shimada's seventeen Type 97 Chi-Ha medium tanks and three Type 94 Ha-Go light tanks. While Shimada attacked the rail bridge with the main force, six tanks and 100 truck-borne infantry under the command of Lieutenant Sadanobu Watanabe were detailed to assault the road bridge.

Watanabe's daring assault was characterised by his decision to dismount from his tank in order to cut the fuse to the demolition charges on the bridge with his sword. In addition to taking both bridges by storm, Japanese tanks also achieved complete tactical surprise at the Cluny Rubber Estate where they caught two British artillery batteries breakfasting by the roadside. A British officer, Colonel Harrison, surveyed the scene after the Japanese tanks had moved on:

> The ammunition trucks and limbers were burning hard, shells were exploding and bullets crackling all over the place. I saw an ambulance bumping drunkenly over the broken ground until it hit a tree and overturned. A subaltern (Lt Hartley?) told me that they had been breakfasting in the rubber 200 yards from the road when someone arrived and reported that tanks had broken through. Major Drought had dashed off to order two guns into action on the road but ... five tanks arrived, halted on the road and strafed the hide ...

In an assault lasting seven hours, a company of tanks, an infantry company, an engineer company and an infantry regiment had succeeded in routing the entire 11th Indian Division. During the battle, Lieutenant Colonel Arthur Harrison came close to losing his life. Notwithstanding his close call with death, Harrison still found it within himself to express his admiration for fellow professionals by stating that, 'Heedless of danger and their isolation they had shattered the division: they had captured the Slim Bridge by their reckless and gallant determination.' The decision to launch a night attack with tanks was indeed both imaginative and bold. It was also a risky manoeuvre, but as Sun Tzu said, 'Opportunities multiply as they are seized.' The risk certainly paid off as the capture of the bridges at Slim River effectively unhinged the entire British defence along the west coast.

An attempt by Lieutenant General Arthur Percival to restore equilibrium on the battlefield met with partial success. Japanese troops advancing down the trunk road from Tampin to Gemas were succumbing to victory fever. As they were not anticipating contact with the enemy, these troops had their rifles tied to the handlebars of their stolen bicycles. Their advance had taken them well ahead of the several hundred strong main column which boasted tanks and engineer trucks. All seemed well, but little did they know that they had been allowed to cross the bridge over the Gemencheh River unmolested. It was only when the main column caught up that all hell broke loose as the bridge was detonated, killing many Japanese troops instantly. Then as the smoke was clearing, B Company of the 2/30th New South Wales Battalion and C Troop of the 2/15th Field Regiment opened fire with rifles and machine guns from concealed positions. Heavy casualties were taken by the ambushed column with at least 500 being killed.

Lacking adequate artillery support, the ambush party was forced to withdraw. By late evening, Japanese engineers had managed to effect repairs on the bridge. The surviving members of the Japanese column were now reinforced with troops from the 11th Regiment and an increasing number of tanks from Colonel Mukaida's 1st Tank Regiment. As the column moved down the road towards Gemas, the leading Japanese tanks came under fire from the 2-Pounder anti-tank guns of the 2/30th New South Wales Battalion. In a short but violent encounter, six out of eight Japanese tanks were destroyed. The plucky Australians under the command of Colonel Frederick 'Black Jack' Gelleghan managed to hold their positions for twenty four hours. Their work done, Gelleghan's troops then withdrew in good order.

Lieutenant General Henry Gordon Bennett commanding Australian forces in Malaya believed that the successful ambush at the Gemencheh River signalled a turning point in the campaign. Indeed he was quoted in the *Singapore Times* as saying that, 'his troops were confident that they would not only halt the Japanese advance, but compel them to be on the defensive.' Bennett's optimism was totally misplaced as he had failed to consider the impact Japanese tanks were making on a campaign that was quickly slipping out of his control. On 16 January, the town of Muar and its harbour fell into Japanese hands following a devastating air-raid which killed or wounded all of the 45th Indian Brigade's officers. The remnants of the brigade retreated down the coast to Parit Jawa located several kilometres away. In the meantime, Japanese troops continued their relentless advance towards Bakri, Parit Sulong and Batu Pahat.

An attempt to retake Muar by a three-pronged advance from Bakri on the following day faltered at the first hurdle when troops of the 45th Indian Brigade were ambushed. Early next morning, General Takuma Nishimura ordered his own three-pronged advance, spearheaded by Captain Shigeo Gotanda's nine Type 95 Ha-Go light tanks. Gotanda wished to emulate Watanabe's daring feat on the Slim River Bridge, and with this in mind he rashly volunteered to lead the charge into Bakri without infantry support. Colonel Masakazu Ogaki who had been placed in charge of the operation had reservations about Gotanda's own mechanised version of the Charge of the Light Brigade as there was always the possibility that the enemy would use their field guns in an anti-tank role. Notwithstanding these concerns, it was decided that Gotanda's attack would go ahead without infantry support as the available troops would be more usefully employed in flanking the 8th Australian Division troops and setting up road blocks to their rear.

In his book *Malaya 1941–1942*, Brian Padair Farrel described the attack going in 'with the force and tempo, but also the overconfidence that had come to characterise their drive down the Malayan peninsula.' To get to Bakri, Gotanda's tanks had to pass through a narrow, moderately high banked cutting with jungle on either side. He may well have noticed the anti-tank gun commanded by Sergeant Charlie Parsons as his tank crested a rise and began the downhill turn towards the cutting. Be that as it may, he certainly did not see the second gun commanded by Sergeant Clarrie Thornton which had been carefully concealed on the edge of the rubber plantation. With cries of 'Tally-ho' and 'There the bastard goes', a mix of armour piercing and high explosive shells ripped into Gotanda's tanks.

It was the high explosive shells which did the real damage as armour piercing rounds tended to penetrate the Ha-Go's thin armour on one side and then come out of the other side. According to Lieutenant Ben Hackney who witnessed the scene, Gotanda's tanks were, 'smashed, set on fire, rendered useless and uninhabitable.' General Yamashita went on record by declaring that Gotanda and his men had met 'a glorious death.' His words were echoed by Lieutenant Colonel Tsuji Masanobu, Chief Operations Officer of the 25th Army who made the following written record:

> Between 16 and 23 January a desperate fight occurred. When the Gotanda Medium Tank Company lost all its tanks, the surviving officers and men had attacked on foot, reaching the enemy artillery position and the Parit Sulong Bridge, where the last of them met a heroic death after holding up the enemy for some time ...

Later the Gotanda Tank Company received a posthumous unit citation. Heaping honours on these men could not however bring them back. Later, a Japanese history of the Imperial Guard would recount their fate in a more prosaic manner by concluding that the lives of brave men had been squandered. Gotanda's attack failed for four reasons. First, he was overconfident and perhaps jealous of Watanabe's success. Second, he chose to take his tanks down an un-reconnoitred road. Third, the attack went in without infantry support. Finally, having been ambushed at Gemas, a similar ambush scenario should have been both anticipated and planned for.

Following the significant tank losses incurred during the actions at Gemas and Bakri, the Japanese tank forces were forced to regroup. As a consequence, Japanese troops continuing the advance into southern Jahore had to do so without tank support until such time as additional armour became available. As the British Commonwealth retreat continued, Japanese engineers continued to perform minor miracles by swiftly repairing blown causeways and bridges.

Meanwhile, on the east coast, the understrength 18th Division had captured Endau on 21 January. Their advance had come at a price, and until reinforcements arrived to restore the depleted ranks, they lacked the strength to break through the Australian positions at Sungei-Mersing. On 26 January, the Japanese convoy sent to reinforce the 18th Division with men and *materiel* was sighted thirty kilometres from Endau. In the ensuing battle, the naval vessels HMS *Thanet* and HMAS *Vampire*, supported in the air by British and Australian Hudson's, Hurricanes and Vildebeests attacked the Japanese transports and their escorts. Despite heavy anti-aircraft fire, the two transports were bombed while the Hurricanes strafed the beaches. No Japanese ships were sunk however, and the landing of badly needed troops and supplies was completed. Now up to strength, the 18th Division began preparing for the assault on Sungei-Mersing, only to quickly cancel those plans when it was discovered that the Australian troops had disengaged prior to their withdrawal towards Singapore.

In the race for the Straits of Jahore, Yamashita's three divisions remained hot on the heels of the retreating British Commonwealth forces. Indeed, in the course of seven weeks his forces had covered approximately 1,100 kilometres of sometimes difficult terrain. His troops had also frequently outfought and outmanoeuvred an enemy whose command structure was displaying increasing signs of weakness. Having said that, even with the 18th Division now at full strength, Yamashita still only had approximately 30,000 troops available. Furthermore, he was constrained by tight administrative margins of supply which meant that he would be forced into taking intelligent calculated risks. His basic plan for the assault on Singapore was to use the same decisive tactics that had brought success in Malaya. Time was of the essence, the supply situation dictating that a prolonged siege was out of the question.

By 30 January, Japanese spearheads had reached Kulai, a mere thirty kilometres from Singapore. The following morning, the melancholy sound of a lone piper of the Argyll and Sutherland Highlanders preceded the final withdrawal onto the island. At 08.15 hrs, the causeway was blown. From his headquarters in the Sultan of Jahore's Green Palace, Yamashita had a fine view of the north coast of Singapore. Addressing his officers on 1 February, he stated confidently that, 'It is a good place to die, surely we shall conquer.' His address was as much based on bluff as his attack plan was. Knowing that artillery shells were in short supply and that he had less than two dozen serviceable tanks available, his objective was to conquer the island fortress as quickly and as cheaply as possible.

Conventional wisdom held that any Japanese assault across the Straits of Jahore would come in the north-east sector, not the north-west. Percival never moved from his assumption that the main focus of the attack would be the naval base located east of the causeway. His orders passed down the chain of command were to defend it to the bitter end. On 20 January, General Archibald Wavell had suggested that the Japanese would choose the denser ground west of the causeway as it was further away from the coastal guns which had been turned around to fire inland. For Wavell it also made no sense that Yamashita would at this late stage abandon his winning strategy by concentrating his forces against the north-east sector.

Shortly before 20.30 hrs on 8 February, the vanguard of some sixteen assault battalions began crossing the Straits in the north-western sector, exactly where Wavell had predicted. By 01.00 hrs, the Japanese troops had secured a firm foothold and were preparing to move forward. By dawn, the 5th and 18th Divisions were across the Straits in their entirety, along with substantial quantities of artillery. During the late afternoon, elements of the Imperial Guards Division (which had not been involved in the main assault) crossed the Strait near the Sembawang Naval Base. Burning oil erupting from the huge fuel tanks caused some casualties among the Guards troops, but the assault continued. Their persistence paid off as an opening created at Kranji allowed the bulk of the Guards units, together with their artillery and tanks to come ashore virtually unopposed. While this was going on, Japanese engineers were close to finishing the rebuilding of the causeway as a wooden structure. A mere two days after the causeway was blown up, Japanese trucks and tanks began crossing the 251st bridge to be completed during the course of the campaign.

With the prize almost within his grasp, Yamashita pressed on with the assault in a calculated show of strength designed to hasten the collapse of morale within the beleaguered fortress. His orders to 'Hit them hard, hit them fast' were brilliantly executed with the penetration by infantry and Ha-Go tanks of the strategically important village of Bukit Timah. Yamashita moved his headquarters to the nearby Ford Motor Factory on 13 February. He then ordered the 18th Division to take the Alexandra Barracks and the 5th Division and the Imperial Guards Division to capture the waterworks at MacRitche and the pumping station at Woodleigh. The resultant fighting was bitter, particularly at the waterworks where Japanese tanks played a decisive role in pushing the British 55th Brigade back to Mount Pleasant Road. Japanese pressure continued to be felt the following day as assaults on Hill 226 and Opium Hill dislodged the determined defenders after hours of hand-to-hand combat. Meanwhile, on the Adam Road, Colonel Shimada's Ha-Go tanks managed to create a bulge through Bukit Brown, towards Caldecott Hill and Adam Park.

The following morning, Percival held a conference with his senior commanders. A last stand would have been theoretically possible, but with the fresh water supply now in Japanese hands and the welfare of a million civilians to consider, the only viable option was surrender. At 16.45 hrs, Percival and several staff officers proceeded by car to Yamashita's headquarters. The so-called 'Tiger of Malaya' was anxious to conclude the formalities quickly before Percival realised how numerically inferior the Japanese were. Following some stonewalling from Percival, Yamashita was no doubt relieved when the surrender was finally signed at 19.50 hrs.

In Japan, the government announced that special 'victory rations' in the form of two bottles of beer, a packet of red beans, (plus caramel drops, candies and cakes for those under thirteen) would be distributed to every family. The press also got in on the act by producing extravagant headlines which left the public in doubt about the scale of the victory. The widely circulated *Asahai Shimbun* carried a banner headline which was typical of the time, it proclaimed: *GENERAL SITUATION OF PACIFIC WAR DECIDED.* General Hideo Ohira, chief of the Press Division expressed his delight at the surrender of the Singapore garrison by stating, 'both the United States and Britain should contemplate the 3,000 years of scorching Japanese history. I solemnly declare that with the fall of Singapore the general situation of the war has been determined.' To underscore their victory in Singapore, a victory parade was held the day following the garrison's capitulation. Japanese tanks, a potent symbol of modernity and state power were a key feature of this parade.

Within a very short time, the tank, as Professor Alaric Searle pointed out in *Armoured Warfare: A Military, Political and Global History,* 'came to be invested with political meaning.' During the First World War, tanks came to represent the qualities that would ultimately ensure victory. Later, as traditional news media was gradually overtaken by newsreels during the inter-war period, both Hitler and Stalin quickly recognised the propaganda possibilities that film offered. Carefully choreographed parades which often included hundreds of tanks were filmed to demonstrate the state's military prowess to the masses. While Japan was relatively late in acquiring tanks, their propaganda value was seized upon very quickly.

The demonstration of Japan's armoured power on 16 February was designed to both humiliate the vanquished colonialists and to communicate a clear message that Japan was now the dominant power in the region. For Britain the catastrophic defeat at Singapore signalled the winding down of the Empire. For Japan, it demonstrated that oriental people were no longer second class citizens. Arguably, one of the most potent symbols of Japan's coming of age was the tank. Although for the peoples of the so-called Co-Prosperity Sphere in the vast swathes of land under Japanese control, the tank became a symbol of oppression.

5

'Let your Great Object be Victory, not Lengthy Campaigns'
Burma, Java, and Guadalcanal

After the major ports in China fell under the control of the Japanese, the 1,126 kilometre long Burma Road became the umbilical cord supplying Chiang's Nationalist forces. Therefore, the Japanese plan for the invasion of Burma largely focused on cutting this vital land based supply route. Burma's raw resources, most significantly the oil fields at Yenangyaung, the cobalt produced at the lead-zinc mines at Namtu and the abundant surplus of rice in the country were also considered as significant factors. The forces allocated to the invasion consisted of General Shojiro Iida's 15th Army which was formed around the 33rd and 55th Infantry Divisions. The only armour allocated to the invasion force was twelve Type 95 Ha-Go light tanks of the 1st Company of the 2nd Tank Regiment (commanded by Lieutenant Okada). These Japanese light tanks had proved successful in China and Malaya, particularly in the pursuit role. Confidence remained high as the inherent vulnerabilities of Japanese armour had been masked by weak opposition. In Burma, that situation would change as the technologically superior British tanks constituted a major threat.

To begin with, it was business as usual for the Japanese as the British Commonwealth forces were routed following a two phased assault launched in mid-December 1941. The attack produced a series of early gains, most notably the fall of Tavoy on 19 January 1942, followed by Kawkareik three days later, and Moulmein on the last day of the month. With British Commonwealth forces in disarray, a retreat across the Sittang River was sanctioned on 19 February. Three days later, the last of the 17th Indian Division troops in the area crossed the bridge before pulling back to Pegu (located ninety kilometres north of the Burmese capital of Rangoon). Here they were reinforced by the 7th Armoured Brigade which was equipped with American built M3 Stuart tanks, affectionately known as 'Honeys.' Although obsolete by European standards, the M3 was to prove itself against the lightly armoured Japanese Ha-Go tanks.

On 6 March 1942, five of Lieutenant Okada's Ha-Go tanks sited in the village of Payagyi came under fire from a much larger force of advancing British M3 'Honeys.' The engagement that followed was carried out in poor weather conditions which hampered visibility and radio communications. In the melee, four Ha-Gos were destroyed by gunfire, the fifth being abandoned by its crew. The Japanese claimed that one M3 had been destroyed. As they had discovered in the recent fighting in the Philippines, this enemy tank was a difficult nut to crack.

Japanese reinforcements continued to arrive in Burma over the following month. Among this second wave of men and *materiel* were the 1st and 14th Tank Regiments which had been transferred from Malaya. Having been spared the attentions of British tanks in Malaya, these newcomers to the Burma theatre undertook test firing against a M3 hulk to establish the effectiveness of their 37 mm tank guns against the enemy tank's armour. The results of the test firing caused consternation among the observers when it was discovered that the Ha-Go was unable to either penetrate the M3 at any angle nor at any range.

During the British retreat towards India, the two tank regiments equipped with M3 'Honeys' were kept particularly busy as a rotating rear-guard. On 27 April, the lead platoon of the Japanese 1st Tank Regiment spotted a group of approximately twenty M3 tanks patrolling in the Ngathet and Shanbin area near Wundwin. Knowing that their armour piercing shells were ineffective, the three Japanese Ha-Gos saturated the lead British tank with high explosive rounds. The tactic worked as the tank was soon engulfed in flames. In the meantime the other British tanks had quickly deployed for action. The battle then intensified following the arrival of the main body of the Japanese 1st Tank Regiment. Despite being outnumbered and outmanoeuvred, the 2nd Royal Tank Regiment (RTR) was able to successfully execute a holding action for the next several hours. During this action, the third rate Japanese Ha-Go tanks fared badly against the second rate British 'Honeys.' Nevertheless, it can still be argued that Japanese armour made a valuable contribution to the campaign by speeding up the rate of the Japanese advance and harrying retreating British Commonwealth forces.

Meanwhile, the tentacles of the ever expanding Japanese empire continued to strangle all opposition. In the Dutch East Indies, resistance collapsed more quickly than the Japanese High Command had expected. British North Borneo surrendered on 19 January 1942, followed quickly by Timor on 10 February and Sumatra on 28 February. These whirlwind advances that had left Java 'almost isolated' served to embolden the high command to advance their schedule for the invasion of the sixth largest island in the world. The utter hopelessness of the Allied position in Java was described by David Thomas in *Battle of the Java Sea:*

> The end in Java was now very near. The enemy vice was ready to tighten around the island. No force—naval, air, or military—had been able to resist the Japanese advance for more than hours at the very best. Any successes on the part of the Allies had been as mere pinpricks compared with the vastness of the conquests the enemy had made in so short a time. Everything seemed to fall before the invaders, demonstrating the utter unpreparedness of the colonial powers to defend themselves and their colonies in the face of determined attack … The poached egg flag of Japan fluttered over nearly every Allied port and town in the South-west Pacific theatre. Only Java had so far escaped conquest—and her days were numbered.

In his headquarters, perched high in the mountains of central Java, General Wavell was highly pessimistic about the defence of Java. Four days after the Japanese Invasion force had left Can Ranh Bay in Indochina, Wavell sent a signal to Churchill which unequivocally pointed to the hard times ahead:

> I AM AFRAID THAT THE DEFENCE OF A.B.D.A. AREA HAS BEEN BROKEN DOWN AND THAT DEFENCE OF JAVA CANNOT NOW LAST LONG … ANYTHING PUT INTO JAVA NOW CAN DO LITTLE TO PROLONG THE STRUGGLE: IT IS MORE A QUESTION OF WHAT YOU WILL CHOOSE TO SAVE … I SEE LITTLE FURTHER USEFULNESS FOR THIS H.Q.…

With few aircraft left after the disaster in Malaya, it fell to Lieutenant Admiral Conrad Helfrich's combined fleet of American, British, Dutch and Australian ships to confront the Japanese. Despite putting up a valiant fight, Helfrich's force (commanded by Rear Admiral Karel Doorman) was destroyed in what was perhaps the most decisive Japanese naval victory since Tsushima in 1905.

The defeat of the Allied naval forces in the Battle of the Java Sea, left the island open to invasion. However, the accelerated invasion timetable placed the whole Java operation at considerable risk as plans to achieve air supremacy over the Java Sea and Java itself depended upon capturing the airfields in South Sumatra, South Borneo and the Celebes intact. The anticipated intact capture of the valuable facilities proved to be woefully over-optimistic. As a consequence, the invasion force 'had to set sail for Java before the air force had been able to strike the decisive blow for the island.' Therefore, the decisive blow would have to be struck on land by General Hitoshi Imamura's 16th Army.

Imamura was in overall command of two major units. The Western Force comprised of the 2nd Infantry Division and the 3rd Mixed Regiment was based at Cam Ranh Bay in French Indochina. The Eastern Force made up from the 48th Division and the 56th Infantry Group was based in the Sulu Archipelago in the south-western Philippines. Tank support for the operation was fairly substantial. The Western Force was able to call on twenty one Type 97 Chi-Ha medium tanks, sixteen Type 97 Te-Ke tankettes and ten Type 95 Ha-Go light tanks. The Eastern Force had at its disposal ten Type 97 mediums, ten Type 95 light tanks, twenty four Type 97 tankettes and five captured M3 Stuarts. Many of these tanks would go on to play a significant role in the subsequent land campaign.

On 1 March 1942, Japanese troops began disembarking from their transports at three landing points. The main force comprising of the 2nd Division and two companies from the 2nd Tank Regiment came ashore at Merak, located on the north-western tip of the island. Imamura experienced some difficulty in 'keeping a grip on his sub-commanders' after ships in his convoy had been hit, 'probably by friendly fire.' During the landings, Imamura lost all of his communications equipment and as a result was isolated from the other widely dispersed landing groups for several days. Nonetheless, the operation went ahead as planned as Imamura had already considered this possibility and was therefore ready to give his subordinates a certain degree of latitude with regard to making command decisions.

On the day of the landings, Imamura set up his headquarters at Serang. He ordered the 2nd Infantry Division to be divided into three detachments. The Nasu Detachment under the command of Major-General Yumio Nasu was tasked with capturing Buitenzorg and cutting the enemy off from their line of retreat from Batavia to Bandoeng. The Fukushima Detachment commanded by Colonel Kyusaku Fukushima and the Sato Detachment under Colonel Hanshichi Sato were tasked with advancing towards Batavia via Balaradja and Tangerang. Lieutenant-Colonel Noguchi's 2nd Reconnaissance Regiment was given the task of locating suitable river crossing points and assessing the strength of enemy opposition. The regiment was also split up into three groups. The 'K' Advance group equipped with five Type 97 tankettes was ordered to seize the bridge at Kopo. The 'Right' Advance group was tasked with using its five tankettes to capture the bridge at Rangkasbitoeng, while the 'Left' Advance group was given instructions to use its three tankettes to take the bridge at Pamarajan.

From the start, luck did not appear to be on the side of the 'K' Advance Group as the commander's tankette ran over a mine when his unit entered Serang. Having survived the explosion, the commander was determined to fulfil his mission, only to discover that the bridge at Kopo had already been destroyed by Dutch troops. Meanwhile, the 'Left' Advance group appeared to making better progress as the commander's tank disabled a Dutch armoured car and prevented defending troops from detonating the bridge with explosives.

On 2 March, the Reconnaissance Regiment's tankettes came under heavy fire from defenders manning an anti-tank barricade at Balungan. While the tankettes held the defenders in check, the main body of the regiment performed a successful flanking action which forced the defenders to withdraw. The tankettes forming the armoured spearhead of the regiment continued their advance the following day. The forward momentum of the advance then experienced a temporary check when the tankettes of the Nasu Detachment came under heavy fire from American and Australian troops near Leuwiliang. The detachment came under further fire when crewmen from the lead vehicle dismounted in order to locate a suitable place to cross the Tjisadane River.

That same day, the Shoji Detachment occupied Soebang in the early hours of the morning after having successfully completed their mission in capturing the airfield at Kalidjati. Colonel Shoji's was no doubt elated by his achievement, and it was perhaps his vanity and overblown pride which then contributed to his failure to detect the counter-attack launched by two hundred and fifty Dutch troops and twenty Marmon-Herrington light tanks at 11.00 hrs that morning. This hastily improvised attack initially went well, with some Dutch tanks penetrating as far as the outskirts of the airfield, however, now fully alerted, Shoji's men put up fierce resistance, forcing the Dutch to withdraw.

The stout defence and spirited counter-attacks mounted by Allied troops held back the Japanese advance for a full day. On 4 March, Lieutenant-General Hein ter Poorten commanding Allied forces in South-East Asia ordered a withdrawal towards Bandoeng. Spotting an opportunity, Colonel Shoji made an independent decision to change the line of advance of his detachment. By employing his tanks as an armoured spearhead in order to penetrate the region north of Bandoeng, Shoji hoped to earn martial glory by cutting-off the retreat of Dutch forces. While Shoji's superior was not entirely happy with his 'self-willed' subordinate, there was really little he could do, given his inability to effectively control his widely dispersed forces on Java's vast battlefield. It is interesting to note that in Shoji's subsequent pursuit operation, his tanks and lorried infantry worked in close cooperation with the 3rd Air Brigade whose full strength was devoted to supporting his detachment.

In the meantime, the Japanese advance which had temporarily stalled at the Tjisadane River was able to develop momentum again after troops effected a crossing on rafts. With the Allied defence in tatters, the Japanese advance gathered speed. On 6 March, Major Mitsunori Wakamatsu's and Major Masaru Egashira's units were ordered by Shoji to attack Dutch forces stationed on and to the west of the main highway leading to Bandoeng. By late evening on the following day, the two units had penetrated as far as the northern suburbs of Bandoeng. Elsewhere, the advance made equally rapid progress with the Nasu Detachment capturing Buitenzorg after a tough fight. As Allied troops pulled back, the tankettes of the Nasu Detachment continued to harass them as they passed through Tjiandjoer and Tjimahi. It was during the course of this pursuit that news arrived on 8 March confirming the surrender of the Allied forces. There is no doubt that Japanese tanks played a significant role in this campaign as they served to unbalance the defending forces, particularly during their withdrawals. Little did the Japanese High Command know but their momentum was about to be shattered. Admiral Yamamoto had told the Emperor that Japanese forces would 'run wild' for a year before being held in check by the superior forces of the Allies. In the event, that check came sooner than had been anticipated.

The stunning American success at the Battle of Midway in June 1942 in which four Japanese aircraft carriers were sunk, provided an opportunity for the Allies to seize the strategic initiative. The target for the first major counter stroke was the Solomon Islands as news had reached Washington that the Japanese had not only taken Tulagi, but had also begun construction of an airbase on the nearby island of Guadalcanal. Operation Watchtower, the American plan to capture Guadalcanal was conceived by Admiral King. The plan was to be executed on a shoestring budget as resources for the operation were somewhat lacking. During the early stages of the American counter-offensive, the Pacific Theatre faced stiff competition for troops and resources as the 'Germany first' policy largely dictated the allocation of precious war supplies.

On 7 August 1942, elements of the 1st US Marine Division assaulted Tulagi, Gavutu and Tanambogo. The 886 Japanese defenders resisted fiercely, killing 122 Marines before they were eventually overwhelmed. Meanwhile, on Guadalcanal, General Vandergrift's Marines achieved complete tactical surprise when their landings between Koli Point and Lunga Point met minimal resistance. Advancing inland, the Marines secured the airfield and began to stake out claims further inland. Having been taken by surprise, the Japanese command based at Rabaul responded quickly by despatching a force of twenty six 'Betty' bombers to attack the American naval covering force commanded by Admiral Fletcher. Alarmed by the swift Japanese response, Fletcher withdrew his aircraft carriers, falsely reporting to Vice Admiral Ghormley that they required urgent refuelling. The untimely withdrawal of Fletcher's carriers left the Marines on Guadalcanal vulnerable to counter-attack.

On the night of 8–9 August, the Imperial Japanese Navy (IJN) restored its wounded pride to some degree by severely mauling the fleet and screening force supporting the Marines on Guadalcanal. While it was a moment to savour, the naval battle fought off Savo Island fell far short of being a decisive Japanese victory as it interrupted rather than disabled the American lines of communication. As Marines dug in to face the inevitable attempt to retake the airfield, Japanese troops under the command of Colonel Kiyonao Ichiki were preparing to land at Taivu Point. The unopposed landings served to stimulate Ichiki's dreams of martial glory.

Ichiki was a firm adherent of a doctrine which emphasised 'intense spiritual training and bayonet-led breakthroughs to compensate for opponent's material superiority.' Therefore, he wasted no time in launching an attack against the Marine positions at Alligator Creek. Victory fever had seemingly affected this impulsive commander to the extent that he did not even wait until his full force had assembled. Predictably, the attack was a complete disaster. Ichiki was either killed in battle or committed suicide.

During the battle, the Marines defending Alligator Creek were able to rely on the support of five M3 Stuarts which helped to tip the balance in the Americans' favour. Nevertheless, the Japanese High Command remained determined to retake the island. Between 29 August and 4 September, reinforcements began to pour in following landings at Taivu Point, Kamimbo and Lunga Point. Following the inconclusive Battle of Cape Esperance on 11–12 October in which the opposing naval forces suffered few losses, additional Japanese reinforcements arrived on Guadalcanal, including the 1st Independent Tank Company.

Beginning on 19 October, elements of the 1st Independent Tank Company carried out a reconnaissance of the west bank of the Matanikau River. The tanks returned the following day, but unlike the first day when no losses were incurred, a waiting 37 mm anti-tank gun succeeded in damaging the platoon leader's tank. These probes achieved little other than to alert the waiting Marines. Nonetheless, the advantage still lay with the Japanese as the defending troops had few anti-tank guns in position. Any advantage the Japanese had was however soon lost as they took too much time to muster their forces. Lacking good military maps, the Japanese reinforcements were unable to quickly find their rendezvous points. Consequently, the attack which was due to commence on 19 October was delayed for several days.

The attack was eventually launched during the afternoon of 23 October. Of the ten Type 97 medium tanks and the two Type 95 Light tanks landed nine days earlier, eleven were committed to the assault. Lack of spares had ensured that one Type 97 with a damaged idler wheel was effectively *hors de combat*. More misfortune was to follow when Captain Yoshito Maeda's command tank developed engine trouble. It was a bad omen for a mission that Maeda was convinced would be his last. His pessimistic outlook was not altogether without foundation as his commanding officer Major-General Tadashi Sumiyoshi was an artillery specialist who knew next to nothing about the employment of armour. Sumiyoshi's order for Maeda's tanks to cross the sandbar at the mouth of the river without artillery or infantry support was no more than an invitation to mass suicide.

Maeda's small tank force attacked in two waves. Almost immediately, heavy artillery fire scattered the advancing infantry, leaving the tanks alone and totally unsupported. The difficult terrain formed by the soft river sand meant that 'the tanks would be channelised, unable to manoeuvre.' The narrow sandbar restricted the tanks to single file movement, making them easy meat for the American 37 mm anti-tank guns. Maeda's gloomy prediction proved correct as he was killed when his tank was destroyed by a shell as it approached the river crossing point. The attack so rashly ordered by the commander of the Sumiyoshi Force was a debacle, Gordon L. Rottman commenting that, 'The twelve tanks, delivered to Guadalcanal with so much effort, other than the two dead and eleven wounded Marines, contributed absolutely nothing to the Japanese offensive.' The failure of Japanese tanks on Guadalcanal can be attributed to Sumiyoshi's decision to launch the 1st Independent Company's inadequately armoured machines against prepared enemy positions located on an obvious approach route across difficult terrain. It was clear that lessons needed to be learned, but would they be learned in time?

6

The Imitation Game
German Influences on
Japanese Doctrine and Tank Design

In 1940, Japanese observers were awestruck as they witnessed the destructive power of the German *Blitzkrieg* in Europe. These developments in modern warfare were then closely studied by the Japanese command in Manchuria who continued to plan for the anticipated conflict with the Soviet Union. In April 1941, the Japanese tank forces were officially freed from their traditional infantry support role when they became a separate entity within the overall force structure of the IJA. The first chief of the independent tank branch was General Shin Yoshida, a cavalryman, whose appointment demonstrated that a strong element of conservatism remained within the Army. Three months after Yoshida took up his post, the Mechanised Army was officially formed by order of the Imperial General Headquarters. One of the tasks of this new formation's headquarters was to conduct the study and implementation of combined-arms warfare. The substantial tank groups, anti-tank formations, artillery, anti-aircraft, and engineer units allocated to the Mechanised Army were intended to create a balanced force structure capable of independently operating in the field for extended periods.

In the event, the reality never came close to matching the intention, as the Mechanised Army had a very short lifespan. Even before the formation of the Mechanised Army was announced, the 1st and 2nd Tank Groups had been disbanded in order to provide the nucleus for the first tank divisions to be raised by the Kwantung Army. The 1st Tank Division *Taku* activated at Ningan in Manchuria in June 1942 was comprised of the 1st Tank Brigade (1st and 5th Tank Regiments) and the 2nd Tank Brigade (3rd and 9th Tank Regiments). The 2nd Tank Division *Geki* activated at Kungchuling in Manchuria consisted of the 3rd Tank Brigade (6th and 7th Tank Regiments) and the 4th Tank Brigade (10th and 11th Tank Regiments). Significantly, the manpower strength of each tank regiment was almost doubled during this period. Furthermore, the large increase in officers meant that some of the lingering issues with tactical command and control capability could now be addressed.

By following the German example, the Japanese aimed to forge their tank divisions into combined-arms formations backed up with balanced support. To this end, tank divisions also included 'a motorised infantry regiment, a reconnaissance battalion, an anti-tank battalion, a field artillery regiment, an anti-aircraft battalion, an engineer battalion, a maintenance battalion and a transport regiment.' On paper, this divisional organisation structure looked impressive, but once again the intention never quite matched the reality as Japan's limited industrial base could not supply the necessary vehicle compliments for each new division. The motorised infantry was meant to be equipped with the Type 1 Ho-Ki armoured personnel carrier (APC) and the Type 1 Ho-Ha halftrack, both very useful vehicles, but ones only produced in limited numbers by Hino Motors. Only seventeen of the new APCs ever reached the 2nd Tank Division, therefore lorried transport remained the primary means of mobility for infantry attached to the new mobile units. Japanese industry was simply not up to the task, meaning that the German panzer grenadier concept which involved troops advancing alongside the tanks in specialised vehicles was impossible to emulate.

Equipping the supporting arms and services remained an issue throughout the war. This meant that mobile artillery continued to consist largely of towed guns. Advances in design and technology remained far ahead of Japan's industrial capacity with the result that much needed vehicles such as the Ho-Ro self-propelled-gun (manufactured by Mitsubishi Heavy Industries) only began to appear in very limited numbers in 1944. Japan's limited industrial base also meant that tank maintenance and repair remained a problematic issue throughout the war. The root of the problem lay in the failure to produce sufficient quantities of heavy recovery vehicles, specialised equipment and essential spare parts. This serious oversight resulted in fateful consequences as Japanese tanks were often required to operate in difficult terrain which placed additional strain on both man and machine.

The raising of the first tank divisions did not produce any increase in overall strength as Japanese production had already reached a wartime peak. The limited numbers of newer or improved tank models being produced gradually replaced the older models whose obsolescence had been clearly demonstrated in the first encounters with Soviet tanks in 1939. Nevertheless, these organisational changes were seen as being beneficial in terms of improving efficiency. In December 1939, the 3rd Tank Division *Taki* was activated in Baotou, China. This division was comprised of the 5th Tank Brigade (8th and 12th Tank Regiments) and the 6th Tank Brigade (13th and 17th Tank Regiments). The structure of this division was more or less identical to the divisions that had preceded it, meaning that it had the same paper strength, but also the same weaknesses. It would be the last formation of its type created until the 4th Tank Division *Hagane* was activated in Chiba, near Tokyo for the defence of the home islands.

In September 1942, the 'Notification of Armour Operations' was issued. This document set out a doctrine more in line with the modern concepts used by their German ally which emphasised that tanks were the main offensive force. Infantry units which up to now had played the leading role were now to support the tanks by carrying out reconnaissance, clearing the enemy from their forward positions and securing the flanks. Artillery and anti-tank units were also instructed to work closely with tank formations by neutralising enemy artillery and destroying enemy tanks. This new armoured doctrine was developed with the anticipated major clash of arms with the Soviet Union in mind, and as such it failed to anticipate the conditions which would be encountered on remote Pacific atolls and the jungle terrain of Burma and New Guinea. Furthermore, the document was deeply flawed as it gave insufficient thought to the use of tanks in a defensive role. For the rest of the war, Japanese tanks would continue to operate with what amounted to a half-completed doctrine.

What comes first, the doctrine or the tank? Certainly, when the first British tanks were developed, they were regarded as no more than curiosities by cavalry-minded officers. Japan's position was different as the tanks existed long before the doctrine which emancipated them from being handmaidens of the infantry was formulated. Part of the problem was that those tanks were now increasingly being shown to be obsolescent. Therefore, Japan was forced to start again from scratch by designing a whole new range of heavier and better armed tanks in an attempt to keep pace with their technologically superior opponents.

While Japanese armoured doctrine was being updated in recognition of the new realities being experienced on the battlefield, the most potent tank available to their tank forces was the Shinhoto Chi-Ha. This rapidly ageing tank was roughly equivalent in combat strength to a German Panzer III from the German *Blitzkrieg* of 1940. Clearly the Allies enjoyed a technological advantage, one which would only become even more telling as the war went on. With the acknowledgement that Japanese industry was incapable of narrowing the technology gap, the Empire of the Sun was obliged to begin negotiations with its most technologically advanced ally for access to modern weapons systems, including the latest tank designs.

On 20 January 1943, the 'Treaty on Economic Cooperation' was signed by the Tripartite Powers. This treaty was the brainchild of Germany's economic envoy to Japan, Dr Helmuth C. H. Wohlthat, whose role as the chief economic negotiator in the Japanese sphere of influence involved promoting the Reich's economic interests by gaining access to the raw materials of those regions under Japanese control. In exchange for these raw materials, Wohlthat was authorised to negotiate the exchange of valuable German war materials and the latest weapons technology. A month later, Admiral Karl Dönitz met with Hitler to discuss the issue of trade with Japan. He suggested using the large and slow-diving Italian submarines as transports as their combat performance was somewhat limited. In exchange for seven German Type VII U-Boats, the Italian Navy (*Regia Marina*) allocated seven submarines for the missions. Within five months, the first fruits of Wohlthat's treaty arrived in Singapore on board the Italian transport submarine *Commandante Alfredo Cappellini*, a converted 'Improved *Marcello* class' submarine that could carry significant loads over long distances.

The Italian submarine had left the port of Bordeaux on 11 May 1943 with a cargo which included mercury, aluminium, welding steel, 20 mm guns, ammunition (including torpedoes), bomb prototypes, bombsights, and blueprints for the latest German heavy tanks and tank destroyers. Having nursed his submarine through the rough seas of the Roaring Forties and the Cape of Good Hope, Corvette Captain Walter Auconi arrived in Sabang, Sumatra on 9 July with engines running on fumes. After refuelling, it took him four days to reach the final destination of Singapore with his precious cargo. This was a remarkable achievement as no other Italian submarine had ever ventured to the Far East before. Soon, Allied command of the ocean would effectively turn any future sorties into suicide missions.

Auconi's daring exploit had served to pique the interest of the High Command in Tokyo. Shortly after departing on his epic voyage, General Hiroshi Oshima, the Japanese ambassador in Berlin made it clear that his government was interested in acquiring an example of a Tiger I tank. On 19 May 1943, the firm of Henschel & Sohn was advised by the German Army Weapons Agency that Japan was interested in purchasing a Tiger I and having it shipped to the mainland as part of their weapons upgrading programme. No doubt, the directors at Henschel were rubbing their hands together at the prospect of what promised to be a very lucrative contract. The champagne corks had hardly finished popping in the boardroom when news came that the Export Consortium for War Material had other ideas. The Japanese export tank would not be newly built by Henschel, but would instead come from their existing stocks. While this decision came as something of a blow, arrangements nonetheless went ahead for a Japanese delegation headed by Oshima to witness a live-fire display of a Tiger I.

The planned display took place on 7 June at Siewerskaja on the Leningrad Front. Colonel-General Georg Lindemann accompanied the Japanese delegation as Senior-Lieutenant Klaus Diehls of the 502nd Heavy Panzer Battalion did an impressive job of putting the Tiger through its paces.

Following this impressive display, Oshima was invited to examine the tank with members of his staff. Oshima was so impressed by what he had seen, that on his return to Berlin, he pressed for the immediate purchase of the Tiger. Having clearly impressed the Japanese Ambassador, Henschel arranged for a further display of the Tiger I in order to set the seal on the deal. On 27 June, Oshima and his staff toured the Henschel Works at Kassel and observed another Tiger I undergoing trials at the nearby test grounds located at Wilhelmstal Castle. That evening, a reception was held for the Japanese delegation at the Henschel family mansion at Falkenberg.

On 19 September, Henschel was informed by the Export Consortium for War Material that the Tiger along with a Panther Ausf D supplied by MAN (Machineworks Augburg Nuremberg) was to be delivered for shipment to Japan from Bordeaux. Unfortunately for the eager Japanese, the plan to transport the tanks hit a snag when disagreements between Henschel and the German Army Weapons Agency regarding the licence agreement for the sale frustrated the process. As the weeks passed by, the Japanese government felt obliged to exert pressure on the Germans in order to expedite the sale. This pressure seemed to have some effect, as by 1 October, Henschel representatives were satisfied that the terms of the sale would protect the company's interests as the export sale price of 645,000 Reichmarks suggested by the Export Consortium was more than double the standard price for a fully fitted out Tiger I. Having agreed on the sale price and conditions of purchase, the Japanese government were very pleased with the deal. Little did they realise that they had been hoodwinked into buying an unused command tank which had been in storage at the Magdeburg–Königsborn Army Tank Ordnance Depot for several months.

The tank selected for export to Japan had been accepted for service as a command vehicle in late August 1943. Shortly afterwards, planned changes to the headquarters companies of the heavy tank battalions rendered the command tanks stored at the Magdeburg–Königsborn facility surplus to requirements. On 14 October, work on converting the selected command tank to a battle tank was completed in the depot workshop. Two days later, the tank was placed on a rail flatcar for transportation to the port of Bordeaux (it is likely that the MAN Panther was included in the same transport). After a series of delays *en route*, the precious cargo finally arrived at the port.

On 23 November, the sales invoice for the Tiger was issued by Henschel to the Showa Tsusho Kaisha Ltd (Japanese agents for the sale). The agreed sale price covered the delivery of, 'One Tiger Model E which was ready for shipment to Japan.' The invoice also included the total cost of production, radio equipment, ammunition, machine guns, gun sights/optics, disassembly/packing, rail shipment, and agents' commissions. Following the breakdown of costs, Henschel received the grand sum of 7,795 Reichmarks which represented 2.5 percent of the sale price. While this was not quite the deal envisaged by the Henschel directors, the Japanese government fared even worse from this one-sided business transaction.

The only real winner from the deal was the German Army Weapons Agency which received 300,000 Reichmarks for the tank, plus a further 249,467 Reichmarks in residuals. By the time that payment from the Japanese government had been confirmed in late February 1944, transportation of the tanks (including the Panther) to Japan by ship or submarine was all but impossible due to the Allied command of the ocean. Even before the payment was confirmed, wartime realities had led the German authorities to authorise the transfer of the Tiger to the 101st SS Heavy Panzer Battalion in Belgium. On 21 September, the transfer of the tank was made official in an order which stated that the Japanese government was making the Tiger available to the German Army 'by way of loan.'

The Tiger and Panther tanks purchased at great cost may never have reached Japan, but at least designers in the homeland had access to the tank blueprints delivered by submarine in July 1943. These blueprints would go on to serve as the inspiration for a whole new generation of Japanese tanks and armoured fighting vehicles designed to nullify Allied qualitative superiority. The Allies had anticipated improvements in Japanese armour. In a pamphlet issued by the United States Office of War Information in 1945 it was estimated that Japanese tanks were 'bound to improve and new models may show considerable German influence.' This estimation was correct in that late-war Japanese tank design had certainly become subject to specific German design traits. Ever since the Type 89B tank was fielded in 1934, the emphasis on Japanese tank design had been on mobility at the expense of armament and armour protection. First encounters with the American Sherman tank had prompted a radical rethink of Japanese tank design. Having said that, it was recognised that designing and producing an entirely new tank would take a considerable amount of time. Therefore it was agreed that what was required was a stopgap tank based on an existing chassis which could be manufactured in quantity while work progressed on a more advanced medium tank design.

The stopgap tank developed in lieu of a more advanced design was the Chi-Nu medium tank. This model represented the final development of the Chi-Ha, a tank which was first produced as far back as 1938. The Chi-Nu was based on the chassis of the Chi-He which was itself a modified version of the Chi-Ha. The modifications made the tank slightly longer and wider than a Chi-Ha, the size difference largely being made up from increased armour protection of between 12 mm and 50 mm in thickness across the various facings. The additional weight from the increased armour was compensated for by the installation of a powerful Mitsubishi Type 100 series V-12 diesel engine which produced a top road speed of thirty-nine kph and an operational range of 210 kilometres. The tank's main armament represented a marked improvement over any previous model and consisted of a powerful tank gun based upon the 75 mm Type 90 field gun. The Type 3 tank gun fitted in the Chi-Nu was noteworthy in that it was capable of firing a 6.6 kg armour piercing round at a muzzle velocity of 670 metres per second. At combat distances of between 100–1,000 metres, the Chi-Nu was shaping up to be a formidable opponent of the Sherman.

Design work on the Chi-Nu was completed in record time (six months) in October 1943. However, production was held back for almost a year due to shortages in materials and shifting war priorities. During 1944, Japanese industry was only able to manufacture a total of 925 tanks, self-propelled guns and other armoured fighting vehicles. Of this total, fifty-five Chi-Nu tanks were produced by Mitsubishi Heavy Industries. This painfully slow rate of production was slightly improved on during the following year when eighty-nine examples were turned out. None of these tanks saw combat as all were reserved for the defence of the home islands. Nonetheless, the Chi-Nu was undoubtedly the most powerful Japanese tank to be produced in significant numbers and would have been a match for the ubiquitous Sherman. In the meantime, increasingly obsolescent tanks were all that was available to help form the backbone of Japanese defences on far-flung Pacific atolls and islands.

7

A Miracle on Tarawa

The Against all Odds Survival of Volunteer Tank Crewman Chief Petty Officer Tadao Onuki

On 17 August 1942, an American attacking force comprised of 222 Marines of the Second Raider Battalion conducted a raid on Makin Island. This remote island situated 160 kilometres to the north of Tarawa Atoll was garrisoned by a small force led by Sergeant Major Kanemitsu. An accidental shot fired by a Marine alerted the garrison who were quickly galvanised into action by Kanemitsu's decisive leadership. After failing to destroy the radio station on Makin, the raiders ran into difficulties disengaging from Kanemitsu's troops. Having extricated themselves, the remaining marines then discovered to their horror that their weakly powered boats struggled to compete with the surf as they sought to return to the waiting submarines *Argonaut* and *Nautilus*.

The raid prompted the Japanese to send substantial troop reinforcements to the Gilbert Islands. Arguably the most important of these islands was Betio, located at the south-western end of the Tarawa Atoll. This small outpost formed the linchpin of the Japanese defence. Here, Rear Admiral Tomanari Saichiro enjoyed the benefits of a natural first line of defence made up of a fringing coral reef which extended seaward to a distance of 1,200 yards in some places. His second line of defence was man made, consisting of a barricade constructed from coconut logs which ran along the edge of the beach and covered approximately half of the island's shoreline. Behind this barricade Saichiro ordered the emplacement of machine guns and artillery protected by more coconut logs, coral, sand, and in some cases, steel. In addition, heavy coastal defence guns sited to cover the anticipated landing areas which had been liberally laced with mines and obstacles.

The High Command in Tokyo was well aware of Tarawa's strategic importance to their overall scheme of defence. Consequently, the decision was made to appoint a younger and more vigorous commander who would take over the island's defensive preparations. Saichiro's replacement, Rear Admiral

Keiji Shibasaki officially took over command on 20 July 1943, although due to delays, he did not arrive on the atoll until September. Nonetheless, once ashore he wasted no time in revitalising the defences on Betio by dividing the days into construction tasks and defensive training. Construction was largely left in the capable hands of Lieutenant Murakami, leaving Shibasaki free to concentrate on what he did best, instilling confidence in his men by training them hard in order to increase their combat effectiveness. His orders to the garrison were simple and to the point, 'Defend to the last man all vital areas and destroy the enemy at the water's edge.'

For the defence of this vital sector on Tarawa, Shibasaki had at his disposal 1,122 well-trained sailors from the 3rd Special Base Force and a further 1,497 from the 7th Special Naval Landing Force. Supplementing these troops were 1,247 Korean labourers from the 111th Construction Unit and 970 labourers from the 4th Fleet Construction Department Detachment. Armoured support on the atoll consisted of a detachment of Ha-Go tanks from the Special Naval Landing Force commanded by Ensign Ohtani. There is some dispute as to the exact numbers employed, but it can be said with some certainty that between seven and fourteen Japanese tanks took part in the defence of the atoll.

One of the tank crewmen making up the formidable defensive force on Tarawa was a volunteer. Following his arrival in June 1943, Chief Petty Officer Tadao Onuki's mood was likely to have been one of confident optimism. Indeed, this mood could only have been bolstered following Shibasaki's arrival as garrison commander and his proud boast that 'it would take one million men one hundred years to take the atoll.' Onuki later recalled how the extensive defensive preparations helped to raise morale:

> Our unit was called No. 3 Yokosuka Special Base Unit, and we spent day after day busy with constructing positions and in battle drill. Air-raids by large enemy aircraft were a daily occurrence, but they never hindered us in any way. We were once raided for 24 hours, by a combined force of fighters and bombers, but they didn't do us any harm, in fact they very effectively raised our morale. Here and there on the island we built some really tough positions making skilful use of the natural features of the terrain. The construction went on without a break, night and day. Our tank unit was completely combat-ready and preparations for the encounter battle went ahead.

As the pre-invasion bombardment lifted on the morning of 20 November 1943, Onuki's tank, along with one other emerged relatively unscathed as they were ensconced in an air-raid trench near to the concrete blockhouse which served as Shibasaki's headquarters. The three-man crew of a third tank were seriously wounded by flying shrapnel as they had failed to secure the observation slit on their vehicle. When it was clear that the bombardment had lifted, Onuki left his tank in order to get new orders.

There was precious little respite for the defending troops as soon after the bombardment ceased, American Amtraks laden with Marines began to pour towards the beach. The troops aboard these lumbering tracked amphibious vehicles did not expect to meet any opposition as it was assumed that the naval bombardment had neutralised all of the defensive positions on the atoll. What they did not know was that much of the bombardment had consisted of flat trajectory fire which had simply glanced off the Japanese bunkers, leaving many of the defenders stunned but very much alive. The surviving Japanese defenders roused themselves and extracted a dreadful toll on the advancing Marines. Onuki later recalled the carnage on the beach:

> In the face of fierce ear-splitting small-arms fire, the enemy landing-craft began to run aground, and the US soldiers began to fall into the sea. I think we dampened their ardour, but they had guts and although they received the full impact of our small-arms fire, they crossed the shallows to the shore, and then trod over the bodies of their fallen comrades, one after the other, until they finally managed to install themselves at one end of the island.

During the heat of the battle, Onuki was unable to obtain new orders. Therefore, he took it upon himself to attack the Marines on the beach. After driving approximately 800 yards, he took up position north of the aircraft revetments at the base of the cove. From here, he had a good field of fire towards the beach and the lagoon where the Amtraks were heading. Onuki vividly described the subsequent encounter with the enemy in a memoir published in Japan in 1970. In it he wrote:

> Inside my tank, I poured out shot until the barrel of my gun was red-hot, but it was impossible not to be aware of the threat of the enemy's numbers ... But we moved here and there on the island and gave the Americans something to think about. Hunting for tanks, I burst into the enemy positions and ended up by penetrating deep into them, almost before I knew what was happening. I tried to withdraw, but for some reason, the engine refused to budge. I was frantic, and couldn't find the cause of the stoppage.

It was at this point that Onuki finally received some orders as a sailor pounding his rifle butt on the tank's side gained his attention. The orders passed on by the sailor were clear; Onuki was to withdraw to the command blockhouse. After stamping down on the axle in sheer desperation, the engine spluttered into life.

On his return to the command blockhouse, Onuki was ordered by an officer to be 'the Admiral's eyes' by re-establishing communications with outlying units. But first there was a more urgent task, that of providing covering fire for Shibasaki who was intending to move his headquarters to a position on the south coast. Onuki wrote:

> The situation of the battle was worse and worse for us. The headquarters for Rear Admiral Shibasaki and others had to move from the first command post to the second command post, and our tank was ordered to cover their move. At the time, the tank unit couldn't move, because we hadn't enough fuel, so we acted as gun platforms. When we finished that assignment, I clambered down from the tank. In that instant, shells from one of the enemy's naval guns came down with a shattering roar and burst all around us. My two comrades who were just emerging from the tank were blown to pieces in a split second.

It was more than likely that the same shells were responsible for killing Shibasaki and his staff who had assembled outside the concrete blockhouse in preparation for the move to the new headquarters. The loss of the charismatic Rear Admiral further complicated Japanese command and control problems to the extent that each defending unit effectively fought in isolation.

With the American Marines clinging on to their tenuous bridgehead, now would have been the time for a powerful counter-attack. Had Shibasaki survived he certainly would have done so, but without his guiding hand, a coordinated attack was no longer possible. Instead, each unit continued to resist doggedly, holding the Marines back according to their prearranged defensive strategy. Even so, the Japanese defenders still managed to inflict a very heavy toll on the invaders, killing and wounding approximately 1,500 Marines on the first day. Their position was however becoming more perilous, as on the second day of the invasion, the Marines received valuable reinforcements in the form of a battery of 75 mm howitzers and a handful of tanks. These heavy weapons were then used to devastating effect as they blasted Japanese positions at close range. Thanks to this fire support, the Marines were also able to establish a secure landing area for troop reinforcements and supplies. For the Japanese, losing the battle of men and *materiel* meant disaster, and by the end of the second day, the entire western end of Betio Island was under American control. As the beachheads were expanded, the Japanese defence was split into two groups. A landing was then made on Bairiki Island east of the Tarawa chain to cut off any possible Japanese escape route.

By the third day, the Japanese defenders had been pushed back towards the narrowest part of Betio Island situated to the east of the airstrip. Small pockets of troops also continued to hold out to the west of the airstrip and in defensive positions close to the American Red Beach 1 and Red Beach 2 sectors. That day a defiant radio message was broadcast which said, 'Our weapons have been destroyed and from now on everyone is attempting a final charge ... May Japan exist for ten thousand years.' Onuki recalled these last desperate hours:

We separated into No 1 and No 2 troops and resolved to carry out one final attack. The report of our fight to the finish was sent off to Japan beforehand.

At that time, the number of US troops who had come ashore were several hundred times greater than that of the Japanese who had survived, and bit by bit, they began to encircle us. We were no longer masters of the seas or the skies, we had no food or ammunition left, and there was no longer any hope of a force coming to relieve us. There was only one way ahead for the Japanese on Tarawa, a fight to the finish and total annihilation.

We said goodbye to No 1 Troop as they moved off for their first attack, and those of us who belonged to No 2 Troop waited in the air-raid trenches until the evening hour when the attack was expected. But in the end we were spotted by a keen-eyed enemy pilot who came in to the attack. In an instant, the inside of the trench was turned into an inferno by his bombs and the explosives hurled at us by US troops and by the flame-throwers which poured flame at us before the smoke from the bombing had cleared away. Everything was incinerated.

With his tank immobilised by lack of fuel, Onuki had been condemned to death as a bayonet wielding infantryman in one of the senseless Banzai operations which characterised the final stages of the battle. Such was his fate until a stroke of good luck intervened:

In that burned out trench, where everything was totally destroyed, no human being could have survived other than by a miracle. As it happened, there was a miracle.

I don't know how long it was before I was aware that I was still alive. I could not move my hands or feet freely, and my body felt as if it were being pressed by something heavy. All I was sure of was the fact that I was still alive. Then I regained consciousness completely. I was lying under a heap of blackened corpses, and around me in the trench I could see hands and feet scattered all over. It was a scene of such disaster that, without thinking, I wanted to cover my eyes, even though I was quite battle-hardened by this time.

Of the fifteen of us who had sworn to live or die together, I was the only one left. There was no sign of any of the others, and my insignificant life had only been saved because I had been sheltered by the dead bodies of my comrades. I could feel that there were burns on my face, but I was still not sure if I was all in one piece, and for a while everything went blank. When I came to again, I tried to crawl out of the trench. It was already dark, and all around me everything had gone uncannily quiet. Tarawa felt exactly like an island of the dead ... The sound of guns which had made the whole island shake had completely died away. Had the fighting come to an end? There was no one to give me orders. I was unarmed. I hadn't even a rifle to fight with. There were no comrades to give me comfort or spur me on. How was I going to stay alive on this island which was filled with enemy soldiers? And supposing I stayed alive, there was absolutely no hope of ever going back to Japan. When I thought about it, an indescribable feeling of loneliness pressed in on me, the terror of it almost stifled me.

Onuki survived for three weeks, living off a meagre diet of coconuts, small fish, prawns and crayfish. For a while, he was joined by six other survivors, who like him, had roamed Betio Island in search of food. Such was the paucity of resources on the island that the group was forced to split up in a desperate search for food.

Driven almost to the point of insanity by thirst and hunger, Onuki threw caution to the wind as he roamed along the beach by the water's edge. Inevitably, he was captured by an American patrol. Being practicably insensible to what was going on, Onuki was unable to fight back, stating that, 'by that time, I had absolutely no physical or spiritual strength to resist left in me.' When Onuki went into captivity, he became a member of a very exclusive club in that he was one of only seventeen survivors from the trained troops who had defended Tarawa. Japanese propaganda had led him to believe that prisoners would be executed by the Americans. In his memoir, he recounts how it only slowly dawned on him that this was not the case:

> The destruction of Tarawa at an end, the seven of us who had secretly survived were weak enough to drop when we were transferred to a US Navy destroyer. We were helped and looked after at first, rather than interrogated, and they gave us food. However, since we had resolved that we would be killed sooner or later, when the next day dawned we said to ourselves, 'This is our last day', and then when the sun went down, we thought, 'We've lived one more day today', with some surprise. It was a complicated feeling. Although for the last three weeks we'd had no fear of dying at all, we began to think we'd been lucky, and as we continued to stay alive, life began to seem a desirable thing.

Onuki and the other survivors from Tarawa were later split up. He was transported by ship to Hawaii, and from there to a prisoner of war camp in

Wisconsin. Onuki was in a camp in Texas when he heard about the Japanese surrender in August 1945.

For the Japanese government, the loss of Tarawa confirmed that the Americans had developed the technology and techniques to take even their most strongly defended island fortresses. There were lessons to be learned; most notably that Banzai charges were a senseless waste of men. From now on infantry would not be wasted, but would instead be preserved in order to fight attritional battles in order to wear the enemy down. Unfortunately, lessons regarding the use of armour were overlooked.

During the course of the battle, Onuki's tank was the only one to take on a mobile role. This occurred during the early stages of the invasion when lacking clear orders he acted entirely on his own initiative. The remaining Ha-Go tanks made a minimal contribution to the defence as they were too few in number and were also markedly inferior to the much more powerful American Shermans deployed on the island. During the battle, Japanese tanks were used almost entirely in a static role which rendered the defence essentially reactive rather than proactive. Having said this, there remains a strong argument for supporting the employment of Japanese tanks in this way as the limited room for tactical manoeuvre on Tarawa greatly reduced their effectiveness. Added to which, the overwhelming enemy firepower which could be brought to bear from offshore American naval assets and aircraft made the movement of tanks a very hazardous exercise. Taking all this into consideration, the decision to employ Japanese tanks in a static role on Tarawa was arguably the correct one.

8

The Road to India
The Japanese 14th Tank Regiment's contribution to the Imphal Operation

The Japanese pursuit of British Commonwealth forces to the Burmese–Indian border in May 1942 was eventually brought to a halt by a combination of logistical difficulties and unfavourable terrain. The Japanese forces under the control of Lieutenant General Shojiro Iida had fought well, their advance having been characterised by the frequent outmanoeuvring of British troops. Nonetheless, Iida remained disappointed, particularly so as he recognised that he had only been able to score a partial victory. Following a series of pessimistic pronouncements made by him about the low chance of success of future operations in the region he was recalled to Tokyo. Iida was replaced by Lieutenant General Masakasu Kawabe as head of the newly created Burma Area Army in March 1943. Within a short time he had been persuaded to give his support to one of his more ambitious subordinates, Lieutenant General Renya Mutaguchi. This highly motivated commander had developed a plan to disrupt the British build-up in the Imphal area of India. While Mutaguchi's plan offered some chance of success, it was strongly opposed by the Vice Chief of Staff of the Southern Expeditionary Army who argued that tight administrative margins for supply would render the operation untenable. The Vice Chief's opposition did not prove to be a serious problem for long as he was sacked in October 1943 following a diplomatic incident with the Siamese regarding the ceding of territories. His replacement, Lieutenant General Kitsuju Ayabe was far more optimistic about the prospects for Mutaguchi's plan, and following his visit to the Imperial Headquarters to gain official approval, he received the go-ahead on the strict understanding that it was to be purely a limited offensive.

Given the threadbare state of Japanese forces in Burma, an element of caution was certainly warranted. The only tank formation available for operations in the region at the time was the 14th Tank Regiment. This depleted force had remained in Burma since the successful conclusion of

The Type 89 medium tank was the first successful home produced model. This example was photographed at an open day at the Tsuchira Tank Museum in Japan. (*Courtesy of Megapixie*)

Panzer I Ausf A in Chinese service during the early stages of the second Sino-Japanese war. (*Wikimedia Commons*)

Chinese Panzer I captured following the Battle of Nanking. (*Wikimedia Commons*)

Corps Commander Georgy Zhukov talks with tank crews from the 11th Tank Brigade during the battle against the Kwantung Army at Nomonhan in 1939. (*Wikimedia Commons*)

A Type 89B medium tank crossing a bridge during the advance on Manilla in January 1942. The weight of Japanese tanks had been largely determined by their ability to cross weak bridge structures. (*Wikimedia Commons*)

Left: Type 2 Te-Ke light tanks proved well suited to the reconnaissance role during the Malayan campaign. (*Wikimedia Commons*)

Below: Ha-Go light tanks contributed greatly to maintaining pressure on retreating British-Commonwealth troops during the Malayan Campaign. (*Wikimedia Commons*)

The weak armament of the Ha-Go failed to make much of an impression on the more heavily armoured M3 'Honey' operated by British forces. (*Courtesy of Mike 1979 Russia CC share alike license BY-SA 4.0*)

Type 1 Ho-Ki Armoured Personnel Carrier. (*Wikimedia Commons*)

Above: Japanese prisoners taken on Tarawa. (*Wikimedia Commons*)

Left: By 1944 Japanese resources in Burma were so scarce that captured tanks and even elephants were pressed into service. (*Wikimedia Commons*)

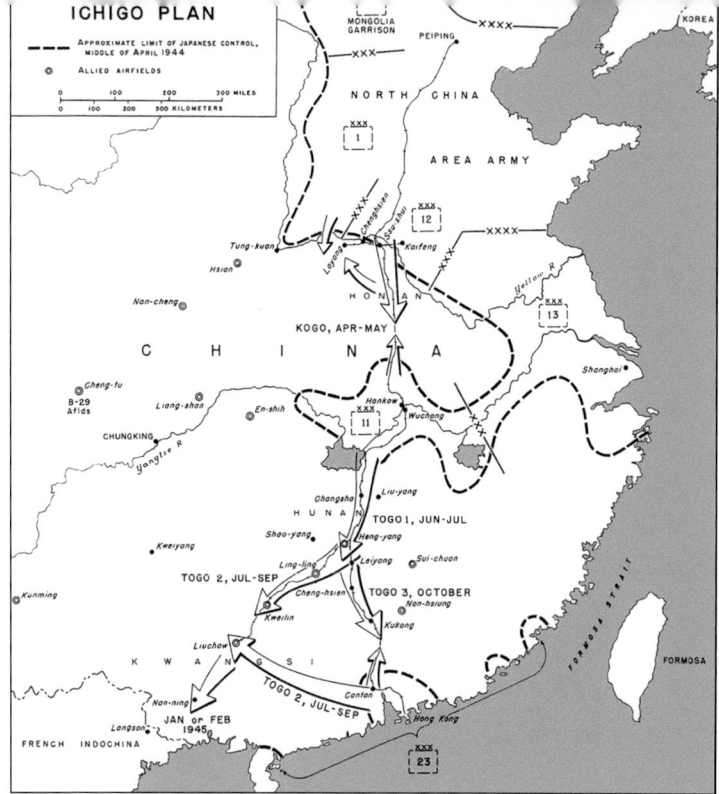

Operation
Ichi-Go.
(*Wikimedia
Commons*)

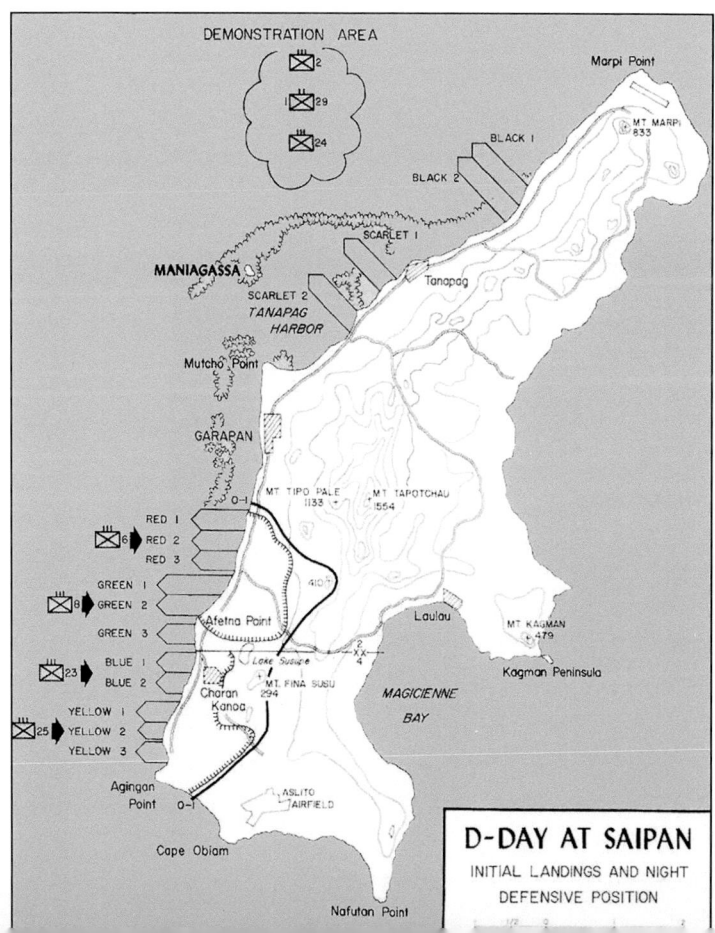

Saipan invasion
beaches.
(*Wikimedia
Commons*)

Above: Marines on Saipan utilising a captured Chi-Ha tank. (*Wikimedia Commons*)

Left: General Douglas MacArthur wades ashore on Leyte. (*Wikimedia Commons*)

Above: Mine Clearance on Leyte next to damaged Japanese Ha-Go tanks. (*Wikimedia Commons*)

Right: A captured Ka-Mi amphibious tank on Leyte. (*Wikimedia Commons*)

A wrecked Te-Ke amphibious tank at Ormoc following the initial battle for Leyte. (*Wikimedia Commons*)

Destroyed Japanese armour on Luzon. (*Wikimedia Commons*)

American armour advances along the Umurbrogol Mountain area on Peleliu. (*Wikimedia Commons*)

A Shinhoto Chi-Ha deployed in an ambush position on Iwo Jima. (*Wikimedia Commons*)

A dummy tank carved from stone on Iwo Jima. (*Wikimedia Commons*)

Right: Map detailing the slow and painful progress of the battle to subdue the island's tenacious defenders. (*Wikimedia Commons*)

Below: This destroyed Te-Ke tankette on Okinawa is being examined by a US Marine. (*Wikimedia Commons*)

JAPANESE POCKET

MARCH 11

NISHI

MARCH 1

Hill 362

Airfield (under construction)

FEB. 24

IWO   JIMA

Hill 382

Airfield No. 2

D-DAY LINE

Airfield No. 1

D-DAY LINE

4 MARINE

PACIFIC OCEAN

JAPANESE POCKET MARCH 11

5 MARINE

3 MARINE (RES.)

5 SCHMIDT

Mt. Suribachi

Scale of Miles

Left: Chi-Nu medium tank production line. (*Wikimedia Commons*)

Below: An extremely rare Type 3 Chi-Nu medium tank on display at the Tsuchiura Ordnance School, Japan. (*Courtesy of Megapixie—Wikimedia Commons*)

A side view of the Type 3 Chi-Nu medium tank. (*Courtesy of Max Smith—Wikimedia Commons*)

Japanese armour on Shumshu. (*Wikimedia Commons*)

Above: Soviet Marines pose by a destroyed Ha-Go light tank on Shumshu. (*Wikimedia Commons*)

Left: Japanese tank crewman. (*Wikimedia Commons*)

the 1942 campaign, but by early 1944 it was clear that its glory days were firmly in the past. Indeed, the regiment was so lacking in armour that its 4th Company had resorted to using M3 Stuarts 'captured from the retreating British 7th Armoured Brigade in 1942.' Notwithstanding the serious logistical deficiencies of the forces allotted to him for his ambitious U-Go operation, Mutaguchi remained largely unconcerned about his prospects for success. His unlimited pride and personal ambition had served to conceive a plan in which the capture of Imphal was only the first stage in a series of thrusts deep into India. Such was his folly.

Mutaguchi's plan was to be carried out in two phases. The opening phase, codenamed Ha-Go was essentially a diversion launched in the Arakan region with the intent of drawing in reserves from the British 14th Army. This would be followed up by the main assault which had Imphal and Kohima as the main objectives. His reasoning was that a successful thrust onto the Imphal Plain between Burma and India would deny the British precious forward bases, and would also serve to cut off the supply route to General Stilwell's Chinese forces in the north.

The opening phase of the operation was launched on 3 February 1944 when a force of 8,000 men under the command of Major General Sakurai set out to infiltrate British positions. After some early successes, Sakurai's force ran into difficulties as the Anglo-Indian forces in the Arakan region stood firm instead of withdrawing as had been expected. Neither Mutaguchi nor Sakurai were aware that the defending forces had pre-planned arrangements for air supply in place, and that with the Japanese threatening to cut them off entirely, these plans had been activated. Everything the defending troops needed was flown into so-called 'boxes', with over 700 sorties delivering 2,300 tons of supplies. At Sinzweya, a British force consisting of Service Corps personnel held out against concentrated Japanese attacks in the so-called 'Admin Box.' During the course of the battle, they were kept supplied by air-drops until relieved by the Indian 5th Division. For the British, the lessons learned in air supply during the Chindit expeditions were now being put to good use. For the Japanese, there were no such luxuries, and throughout the remainder of the war the Emperor's loyal troops continued to subsist on the meagre supplies available to them. Operations were run on a shoestring budget. Everything was in short supply including, food, ammunition, heavy weapons, transport, and significantly, tank support.

The understrength 14th Tank Regiment could only contribute sixty-six tanks to the second stage of the operation. These tanks were of various types, including Type 95 Ha-Go light tanks, Type 97 Shinhoto Chi-Ha medium tanks, captured M3 Stuart light tanks and Type 97 Te-Ke tankettes. On 8 March 1944, the regiment (attached to the brigade sized Yamamoto Force) set off to capture Imphal and Kohima. Meanwhile, the 31st Infantry Division advanced towards Dimapur, the 33rd Infantry Division attacked Imphal from the south, and the understrength 15th Infantry Division attacked Imphal from the north. Two brigades from Chandra Bose's Indian National Army were also available to provide the advancing forces with valuable assistance by acting as covering forces, carrying out reconnaissance, and spreading anti-British propaganda.

To begin with it appeared that the gamble was paying off as Japanese forces made rapid progress. On 20 March the 3rd Company of the 14th Tank Regiment ambushed a mixed British column advancing through the dense tropical forest in the Kabaw Valley. The skilfully executed ambush almost succeeded, but the weak armament mounted on the three Ha-Go tanks was unable to penetrate the side armour of the heavier American built M3 Lee/Grant tanks. Taking advantage of the temporary confusion caused by the ambush, Sub-Lieutenant Hanabusa managed to manoeuvre his captured M3 Stuart tank into position to fire into the rear of one of the Lee/Grants. His spirited attack paid dividends as his 37 mm shells penetrated the engine compartment of the British crewed tank, setting it ablaze. It was though a pyrrhic victory, as during the course of the engagement, all six Ha-Go tanks in Hanabusa's company were destroyed or disabled. It was clear that the M3 Lee/Grant, a tank long since obsolete in the European theatre was a formidable opponent in Burma. The technical balance of power had unmistakably now swung in favour of the Allies.

By the end of the month, Japanese forces had succeeded in interdicting the vital Imphal–Kohima Road. Following this success, the direct assault on Kohima commenced on 4 April. Little did they know it, but their advance was about to run into a brick wall as the British garrison of 1,500 men defending Kohima had orders to hold fast until relieved. Five days of continuous fighting then reduced the battle area to a contest for possession of the District Commissioner's tennis court. Grenades replaced tennis balls as men fought shoulder to shoulder, hand to hand. Neither side gave, nor expected any quarter, and as the grim battle raged on, the position of the defending troops became ever more desperate.

Elsewhere, the fighting was equally as ferocious, particularly that involving the Yamamoto Force which was engaged in an attempt to get past the British positions around the Shenam Pass/Saddle *en route* to Imphal. Here too, the British defences held firm amid conditions that had begun to closely resemble the topography of a First World War battlefield. Japanese tank support was desperately needed in order to break the deadlock. The only support available was the 14th Tank Regiment which was advancing with elements of the 33rd Infantry Division from Moleh through jungle topped hills and monsoon lashed positions. At Tengnoupal, south-east of Imphal, a successful holding action by British troops on 20 April ensured that these much needed Japanese armoured reinforcements never arrived. The unsuitable terrain consisting of hilly, dense tropical forest had also proved to be an obstacle as it had greatly restricted movement. Considering any further attempt at advancing to be a futile exercise, Colonel Nobuo Ueda ordered his tanks to withdraw. Ueda's superior, General Yamamoto knew little about armoured warfare and was known to be 'brusque and impatient with his subordinates.' It was therefore inevitable that Ueda would be replaced with a more compliant officer.

In late April, Mutaguchi decided to concentrate his forces on the Bishenpur–Imphal Road in order to fully exploit the progress of the 33rd Infantry division. His plan was to take Bishenpur before moving against Imphal. To achieve this aim he directed the 14th Tank Regiment and elements of the 18th Heavy Field Artillery, the 1st Anti-Tank Gun Battalion, the 67th Infantry Regiment, 151st Infantry Regiment and the 154th Infantry Regiment to reinforce his attacking units. The forty remaining tanks of the 14th Tank Regiment were obliged to complete the 550 kilometre journey through the mountainous Arakan region on their tracks. The tortuous journey to the Imphal Plain took almost a whole month, by which time the fourteen serviceable tanks remaining had missed the main offensive.

Operating with the Ise Detachment in early June, the 4th Tank Regiment took part in the last serious attempt to break through to Imphal. On 12 June a combined infantry–artillery–tank attack succeeded in producing a small lodgement on the eastern bank of the stream at Ningthoukhong. Tank losses were heavy due to the glutinous mud. For the British anti-tank gunners, these floundering machines provided easy targets. This check was sufficient to bring Mutaguchi's forces to a halt as they were too weak to press home their attacks. Mutaguchi was slow to realise that the high tide of his offensive had already been reached. His decision to continue the offensive in the monsoon season, at a time when a collapsing logistical system was no longer able to support the troops in the field characterised the madness that had overcome him. Once again a Japanese commander had been consumed by selfish pride.

In mid-July, orders from Tokyo and operational realities finally forced Mutaguchi to bow to the inevitable. At Ningthoukhong, tanks had to be abandoned as they were held fast in the clinging mud. By the time the retreating Japanese troops reached the Chindwin River, many of them were so weakened by hunger, malaria and dysentery that they drowned attempting to make the crossing. For the Japanese, Imphal was a disaster. Of the original force of 85,000 troops, only 32,000 survived. Of the sixty-six tanks committed to the operation in March 1944, only four were still in serviceable condition by late July. The contribution of tanks to the Burma-India operation was marginal at best, too few were available, and those that were had weak armour and armament. While the 14th Tank Regiment cooperated well with the infantry and artillery in frontal assaults, their machines were wholly unsuited to carrying out wide envelopments through extremely difficult terrain. In the final battles for Burma in 1945, the rebuilt 14th Tank Regiment's Shinhoto Chi-Ha tanks would be totally outclassed by the Shermans of the British 255th Tank Brigade.

9

Breaking the Deadlock

The Japanese 3rd Tank Division's involvement in the Continental Cross-Through Operation in China

In sharp contrast to the Pacific and south-east Asia theatres, the war in China had been characterised by occasional small-scale operations of limited strategic value. Japan had ended large-scale operations in 1938, content to force Chiang to the negotiating table by blockade. The build-up of the American 14th Air force in China during 1943 then considerably altered the balance of forces. Thus the long stalemate was eventually brought to an end. Conscious of the threat posed to the mainland by American bombers, the High Command in Tokyo reluctantly sanctioned the resumption of large-scale operations. Subsequently, plans were drawn up for Operation Ichi-Go, a major undertaking which had four main objectives involving the capture of the American airfields at Kweilin and Liuchow, preventing the enemy moving into south China via India, Burma and Yunnan, establishing a reliable rail-link between Korea and Rangoon, and dealing a crushing blow to Chiang's Nationalist Army. After a number of conferences, the Imperial General Headquarters approved the plan. On 24 January 1944, orders were issued to the commander of the China Expeditionary Army which emphasised the importance of capturing the airfields. The forces allocated to this major operation would be considerable.

The Continental Cross-Through Operation (more commonly known as Ichi-Go) was split into two phases, Operation Kogo, and Operations Togo 1 and Togo 2. Operation Kogo was due to commence in April and was expected to be concluded in approximately six weeks. The main objectives of the Japanese 12th Army in this first phase were to destroy Chinese Nationalist forces drawn from the 1st War Sector Army and the capture and securing of areas south of the Huang Ho and along the Peking–Hankow railway. On completion of their mission, Japanese forces would be transferred by land to the Hunan–Kwangsi operational area. The second phase to be carried out by

11th Army was due to commence in June (Operation Togo 1) and by 23rd Army in July–August (Operation Togo 2). The objectives of the Japanese forces involved was to destroy the Chinese 4th and 9th War Sector Armies. Following the successful completion of their mission, they were then to capture and secure the Hunan–Kwangsi and Canton–Hankow railways.

Preparations for the largest series of operations ever conducted in China were extensive. Japanese engineer units diverted the Yellow River, repaired railway bridges, moved rolling stock to the main Peking–Hankow line, and expanded existing airfields. The forces committed to the operation were commensurate to the scale of the endeavour, and troop transfers from the Kwantung Army and the home islands soon brought the number of units involved to an impressive seventeen divisions. Significantly, the whole of the 3rd Tank Division was allocated to the first phase of the operation. Lieutenant-General Yamaji's force of 255 tanks was largely made up of a mix of older type 97 Chi-Ha mediums and some of the newer upgunned models. It goes without saying that some examples of the ubiquitous Type 95 Ha-Go light tank were also available for the operation. The tank force was split up into three sections, the Dash-Forward (Advance) Group which consisted of the reconnaissance and engineer elements, the Right-Dash Group which was made up of the 13th Tank Regiment, the bulk of the 3rd Mobile Infantry Regiment and half of the 3rd Mobile Artillery Regiment, and the Left-Dash group which was formed from the 6th Tank Brigade, the 17th Tank Regiment, the remaining elements of the 3rd Mobile Infantry Regiment and the remaining half of the 3rd Mobile Artillery Regiment.

On the night of 18/19 April, Japanese troops began to advance across the Yellow River. The spearhead consisting of three infantry divisions, several independent mixed brigades and the 3rd Tank Division crossed into Henan without meeting much opposition. This was mainly due to a serious intelligence failure by Chiang's agents which 'resulted in his total unawareness of the Japanese moving a whole tank division other than infantry units across the Yellow River Bridge'. The Koumintang leader simply could not bring himself to believe that Japan had the resources to conduct operations along the entire length of the rail corridor between Peking and Indochina. This intelligence failure would prove to be a significant contributory factor in the Chinese collapse which followed.

During late April, Japanese spearheads continued to press southward. Chiang had anticipated this move and had assigned his deputy commander General Tang Enbo a division (2000 troops) to defend the city of Xuchang. The defenders, who were led by a young officer from the Whampoa Military Academy fought bravely, but their fate was sealed the moment a company of Japanese tanks broke through the city gates. In a hard fought contest lasting slightly longer than a day, Japanese forces scored a clear-cut victory over the understrength Chinese garrison whose commander committed suicide on 1 May.

Following the capture of Xuchang, the Japanese 12th Army (minus the 27th Infantry Division) wheeled right for the drive towards Luoyang. The 3rd Tank Division and the 4th Cavalry Brigade formed the spearhead which 'launched a blitzkrieg strike along a river valley pointing towards Luoyang.' Lieutenant General Hideo Yamaji then ordered his Dash-Forward (Advance) group to 'advance rapidly on Baisha, ignoring any small Chinese forces encountered en route.' Meanwhile, the Dash-Left and Dash-Right Groups advanced on Linru. On the afternoon of 2 May, the strongly defended town of Jiaxian was attacked by the main body of the 3rd Tank Division. That night, the Reconnaissance Unit carried out a stealthy advance to the west of the town where they then coordinated with the main body of the division to launch an attack in order to drive the Chinese defenders out. By the following day, the Chinese front had all but collapsed, with Tang Enbo's forces 'running for safety into the mountainous areas of western Henan.'

With his defence in disarray, there was little Chiang could do to prevent the swift capture of Linru and Baisha by the Japanese. Fast moving Japanese units were able to push towards the south-west of Luoyang, and then turn around and come back to encircle it completely. In mid-May, the 63rd Infantry Division, reinforced by elements of the 3rd Tank Division attacked the strongly-defended town. The first assault was repulsed, but on 24 May, the capture of the fortified Beimang Mountain rendered any further defence of the walled city untenable. In the meantime, Chiang's communications with his commanders in the area had broken down completely, and as a result his attempts to assemble a relieving force came to nothing. It was therefore a foregone conclusion that Luoyang's fall was could not be delayed for long.

Without the protection of the northern shield provided by the Beimang Mountain defences, Luoyang's garrison could only manage to hold out for one day against the Japanese 63rd Infantry Division and 3rd Tank Division. For Chiang, the Henan battles were a disaster which was soon compounded by General Hu Zongnan's utter failure to stem a limited Japanese offensive aimed at Lingbao. Later Chiang would have three divisional commanders, all Whampoa graduates shot for retreating without permission. Had the Japanese command taken a more flexible approach, they might have seen the opportunity created by the Lingbao offensive to deal a crushing blow to the Kuomintang regime. Instead, they rigidly kept to their timetable, thus giving Chiang the desperate respite he needed.

Japanese tanks played an active part in the first phase of the Ichi-Go offensive. Having concentrated their tanks *en masse*, the Japanese were able to deal a crushing blow to General Tang Enbo's forces which were simply unable to stand up to this sustained mechanised assault. Japanese tank forces also proved to be very effective in the pursuit role during the Henan battles as every time Chiang was able to achieve some semblance of order among his troops, the appearance of tanks would provoke another panicky retreat. While the Chinese forces were in full retreat, the pursuing Japanese tanks faced their own difficulties. The long distances and difficult terrain in the region placed huge strains on engines and tracks which the inadequately equipped maintenance services could not cope with. Consequently, tank serviceability rates throughout the operation were poor, meaning that many tanks would not be available for the second phase, Operation Togo 1.

The second phase of the operation was launched on schedule in late June. Japanese forces involved in the advance towards Guangxi, Guizhou, Sichuan, and Yunnan provinces had been equipped with substantial numbers of motor vehicles and horses. But on this occasion, tank support was limited as only the 3rd Tank Division's 6th Tank Brigade was available for this stage of the operation. The remainder of the division's tanks were undergoing much needed maintenance and as a result would be *hors de combat* for the foreseeable future. The highly mobile force which carried out the southward advance expected to meet stiff opposition near Hengyang, a key strategic point located at the intersection of the Guangzhou–Wuhan and Hunan–Guangxi railways. It was here that the lack of adequate tank support would be most keenly felt.

Having correctly anticipated the next Japanese move, Chiang ordered his commanders to outflank the Japanese before they reached Hengyang. Despite reading Japanese intentions correctly, Chiang soon learned that his own forces had been flanked by the Japanese 3rd and 13th Infantry Divisions at Liuyang. This startling Japanese advance left the defenders of Changsha totally isolated. The Chinese garrison commander General Zhang De-neng ordered a withdrawal which was soon countermanded by the commander of the 9th War Zone, General Xue Yue. The skittish garrison commander then fled, leaving his troops in disarray. For Chiang, the loss of Changsha was a disaster as it brought American confidence in his regime to an all-time low. The 6th Tank Brigade did not take part in the capture of Henan's capital as 'most of its vehicles had been wasted by long continuous marches.' Having missed the most important initial stage of the operation, the brigade finally arrived in Changsha in October, long after the fighting was over. Thereafter, it was largely involved in providing rear area security and protecting lines of communication. The Japanese tanks which should have provided the armoured spearhead for the remainder of the operation were hence turned into mobile sentry boxes.

There was no let up following the capture of Changsha, as the operation continued with a southerly drive culminating in the capture of Guilin, Liuzhou and Nanning. For the Japanese, these victories came at a heavy price as the heavy losses incurred during these battles and the epic forty-seven day battle for Hengyang had severely reduced the combat effectiveness of the 68th and 116th Infantry Divisions. Yet despite the heavy losses incurred, by January 1945, the objectives of the operation had been largely achieved with the capture of American airbases, the infliction of severe casualties on the Kuomintang forces, and the linking up of the occupied territories. While on the surface the operation appeared to have been a great success, the reality was that it failed to bring any great benefits to the Japanese occupiers. This leaves the question, was Ichi-Go really worth all of the effort that went into it?

The answer to the question must be a definite no, as the weakening of Chiang's regime only served to help the Chinese Communists who were poised to fill the political void. Moreover, the linking of the occupied territories following the opening up of rail communications did little to improve the overall situation for Japan as the losses incurred during the operation meant that there were too few troops available to guard lines of communication effectively. As a consequence, in April 1945, only a single train carrying supplies ran on the Guangzhou-Wuhan line. Transportation difficulties were further compounded by American bombing raids launched from Chinese bases in Szechwan Province. It was therefore inevitable that the Japanese would have no other option than to launch a new series of attacks to capture these American airbases.

In early March 1945, the Japanese 3rd Tank Division was assigned to the 12th Army for operations in Hubei Province. Following advances from Lushan, Paoanchen, Shengtin and Shaholin, the Japanese spearhead made contact with Chinese forces on 21 March. On this day, the poor weather that had grounded American aircraft since 12 March finally cleared. The subsequent Bombing raids failed to make an impression on the Japanese columns which moved only under the cover of darkness. Relatively safe from Allied bombing, the advance continued with the capture of the strongpoints at Nanyang and Tengshein effectively dooming the defence of Laohokow which was abandoned on 26 March. Laohokow was the last American airbase to be captured by Japanese forces. The March offensive was also the last time that Japanese tanks participated in a successful offensive operation during the war. From now on, Japanese tank formations would be employed in a strictly defensive role.

10

Carnage on Red Beach
Japanese Tanks Launch a Night Attack in Force during the Battle for Saipan

Following the loss of the Marshall Islands in February 1944, the High Command in Tokyo was faced with a dramatically changed position which necessitated a readjustment of defensive priorities. Three days after the fall of Kwajalein, the Chiefs of Staff and their advisors met at the Imperial Palace to discuss strategy. Admiral Chūichi Nagumo stated that the decisive battle would be fought at sea, an opinion that was immediately challenged by the Army Chief of Staff Field Marshal Hajime Sugiyama who asked, 'If we give you all the planes you want, would this battle turn the tide of the war?' Nagumo could give no such assurance, and consequently the meeting broke up following a compromise agreement which only served to partly satisfy the Army and Navy's requests for more fighter planes. This continual inter-service squabbling produced nothing other than the significant undermining of Japanese defensive capabilities.

On 17 February 1945, amphibious forces under the command of Admiral Chester Nimitz leapfrogged from Kwajalein to Eniwetok, bypassing four atolls on which Japanese air bases were situated. That day, and on the following day, the naval anchorage at Truk in the Carolines was attacked by air. These raids were a major blow to the Japanese as their losses amounted to seventy aircraft and 200,000 tons of shipping. The raids also seemed to magnify the danger of the rapid American advances in the Central Pacific, so much so that Prime Minister Hideki Tojo's friend and advisor Kenryo Sato suggested that, 'We should withdraw to the Philippines, and there gamble on the final decisive battle.' Tojo was unimpressed, retorting, 'Last year at an imperial conference, we made the Marianas and Carolines our last defence line! Do you mean to say that six months later we should give them up without a fight?' Sato's intervention led to Tojo taking a firmer line by requesting the Army Chief of Staff's resignation.

On 21 February, Tojo assumed the role of Army Chief of Staff himself, and at the same time replaced Navy Chief of Staff Admiral Osami Nagano with the Navy Minister Shigetaro Shimada. Any illusions by Sato that this change in leadership heralded a change in policy were however soon shattered, as within hours of making the changes, Tojo telephoned to state categorically, 'I intend to defend the Marianas and Carolines.' More personnel changes followed as the entire command structure in the central and western Pacific areas was reorganised. Admiral Nagumo was sent to Saipan to command the newly created Central Pacific Area Fleet. Technically, as the highest ranking officer, he was in charge of all forces in the area, including those of the Army. In reality, continuing inter-service rivalries reduced his role to that of a mere figurehead.

In late May, the 43rd Infantry Division sailed from Tateyama in Japan for Saipan. The first echelon of the division sailed without incident, but the second carrying the 118th Infantry Regiment was intercepted by American submarines which sank two thirds of Convoy 3530. The survivors, who had been plucked from the water, crowded the decks of the remaining transports. Some of them were badly wounded, and many others had lost their weapons and equipment. The division was so weakened by the submarine attack that one staff officer did not think that it would be ready for combat operations until November.

The island's defences too were weak due to the building materials needed for fortifications being in desperately short supply. Cement, barbed wire and timber had been sent by ship, but very little had arrived due to interdiction by American submarines. Like the troop transports, these precious cargoes now rested at the bottom of the sea. The defenders would have to make do with what they had to hand. Some defences had been constructed, most notably those on the southwest coast from Flores Point to Agingan Point which 'bristled with artillery, machine-gun positions, pillboxes, and entrenchments.' Building materials may have been in short supply, but an even more precious commodity was time, and for the defenders of Saipan it was running out fast.

Lieutenant General Yoshitsugu Saito, commanding 31st Army on Saipan had 31,629 troops at his disposal. His predominantly infantry based force was supplemented by the 3rd Independent Mountain Artillery Regiment, the 9th Independent Mixed Brigade, the 25th Anti-Aircraft Artillery Regiment, the 14th and 17th Mortar Battalions, and the bulk of the 9th Tank Regiment (1st Tank Division). The forty-seven tanks on the island formed a mobile defence force sited in readiness for the expected landings on Saipan's central or lower west coast. Most of the regiment's thirty-one Chi-Ha medium tanks, four Shinhoto Chi-Ha mediums, and twelve Ha-Go light tanks were positioned near Garapan and Tanapag Harbour. Only one company was left to guard the beaches at Charan Kanoa. Despite the obvious shortcomings of his defensive forces, Saito remained bullish, announcing on 10 June that he was ready to confront the Americans on the beaches.

The following day, American carrier based sorties against the Marianas were carried out by some 200 *Hellcat* fighters. Thirty-six Japanese aircraft were shot down in aerial combat and approximately one-third of all the land-based aircraft on Saipan, Guam, Tinian and Rota were destroyed. There were more attacks on 12 June with a total of 468 sorties being flown. The increased American air activity in the area convinced Admiral Soemu Toyoda that the invasion of Saipan was imminent. He subsequently authorised the execution of Operation A-Go which aimed at destroying the American carriers in a pincer movement carried out by Admiral Jisaburō Ozawa's 1st Mobile Fleet. Ozawa planned to supplement the power of his carrier force with a force of 500 land-based aircraft.

The A-Go operation was doomed from the start, as the land-based aircraft Ozawa was relying on to supplement his carrier-borne strike force had been largely destroyed in a series of devastating attacks. Nonetheless, he decided to press on with the operation, thus turning it into a classic carrier confrontation. His unbalanced force of new carriers, hybrid carriers, and light carriers came up against the powerful Task Force 58 consisting of the modern *Essex* and *Independence* class carriers. The combat-hardened American veterans piloting their agile and robust *Hellcat* fighters outnumbered the inexperienced Japanese flyers by two-to-one. In the ensuing battle, Ozawa's forces were outclassed qualitatively and quantitatively in the air.

American radar picked up all four of Ozawa's air attacks on 19 June. As a result, not one of the first wave of attacking Japanese aircraft made contact with the American carriers. The second wave was more successful, but their aircraft were easy meat for the American pilots who shot down ninety-seven out of the 107 dispatched. It was open season with regards to the third and fourth waves too, the combat proving so unequal that on board the American carrier *Lexington,* a pilot was heard to exclaim, 'Hell, this is like an old-time turkey shoot.' The destruction of 395 Japanese aircraft in the air-combat on 19 June has since been known as 'The Great Marianas Turkey Shoot.' The success of American naval forces in the Battle of the Philippine Sea meant that landings on the Marianas could now go ahead without interference by the Japanese Navy. This success, combined with the effective neutralisation of the Japanese fleet anchorage at Truk meant the date of the landings could be brought forward to the 15 June. For the semi-prepared defenders of Saipan this spelt disaster.

The pre-invasion bombardment of the island's defences proved largely ineffective, and along the six-and-a-half kilometre invasion front centred on the little town of Charan Kanoa, enough Japanese defenders survived to inflict terrible casualties on the advancing Marines. Japanese gun positions and machine-gun nests had to be neutralised one-by-one, meaning that the invasion would be a long drawn out battle of attrition. Knowing this, Saito remained optimistic, even after a stray American shell killed half of his staff. He also recognised that while considerable numbers of Marines had got ashore, they still faced problems in securing their beachhead. Having carefully appraised the situation, Saito sent a message to Tokyo explaining his intentions:

AFTER DARK THE DIVISION WILL LAUNCH A NIGHT ATTACK IN FORCE AND EXPECT TO ANNIHILATE THE ENEMY AT ONE SWOOP.

From the beginning, Saito's attack plan was bedevilled by problems. As his units were widely scattered about the island, he was unable achieve a sufficient concentration of forces for a decisive battle. Notwithstanding, he decided to go ahead with the attack with the forces available.

To bolster the morale of the attacking troops, Saito had planned to send them off personally. In the event this it was not possible as he had become separated from his remaining staff. Movement around the assembly point had attracted American artillery which then began to lay down an accurate barrage. During the ensuing chaos, Saito disappeared, and was presumed dead. Meanwhile, Captain Nario Yoshimura's 4th Tank Company and accompanying infantrymen waited on the hill above Charan Konoa for orders. In the early hours of the morning, news came which indicated that Saito had 'burned to death in a sugar-cane fire.' Major Takashi Hirakushi was sent to find Saito's body, while in the meantime the much delayed attack went ahead.

Tank engines spluttered into life, 'drive wheels turned, and tracks clanked' as the small armoured force headed down the hill. The infantry could not keep up with the fast moving tanks, and was soon left behind. Before the Japanese armour had even covered three-quarters of a kilometre, the lead tank was hit by a shell, bringing it to a halt. But the tanks rolled on, some becoming bogged down in swampland to the east of the town. This delay allowed the infantry to catch up, and once the tanks broke free off the morass, a combined infantry-tank assault was launched against the American positions. Heavy gunfire, including 5 inch shells from offshore destroyers helped to bring the attack to a standstill. The Japanese force regrouped time and time again to launch a series of piecemeal attacks which failed to break through the Marine's defence. Only three of Yoshimura's tanks survived this series of bloody encounters.

Rumours of Saito's death proved to be premature as somehow he had managed to make it back to his command post unscathed. He still had hopes of inflicting a telling blow on the American forces who were still busy consolidating their positions. In reality, the time for such an attack had already passed, and it was perhaps with this in mind that Saito ordered a more realistic attack which was limited to eliminating enemy troop concentrations situated near to the radio station on the outskirts of Garapan. This more limited objective reflected the current balance of forces on the island. The goal should have been achievable, but Saito soon discovered that even his more modest plan was beset with problems. Extensive damage had been inflicted on Japanese communications during the opening stages of the invasion, thereby rendering effective communication with the attacking forces almost impossible. In addition, the orders given to Colonel Yukimatsu Ogawa commanding the 136th Infantry Regiment and Colonel Hideki Goto commanding the 9th Tank Regiment were, to say the least, rather confusing:

> The centre force [136th Infantry Regiment] will attack the enemy in the direction of Oreai with its full force. The tank unit [9th Tank Regiment] will advance SW of Hill 164.6 after the attack unit ... has commenced the attack. The tank unit will charge the transmitting station and throw the enemy into disorder just before the penetration of the attack unit into this sector.

To comply with the above order would have required the tank force to have been in several places at the same time. This was clearly an impossibility, and as Major Carl. W. Hoffman later noted in his historical monograph, 'If the two Colonels read this order with furrowed brows, it is no wonder.'

Forty-four tanks were available for the attack. This total included the fourteen tanks from the 3rd Tank Company, fourteen from the 5th, seven from the 6th, six from headquarters, the three survivors from the previous attacks, and the several Ha-Go and Ka-Mi tanks belonging to the Special Naval Landing Force. The attack which was due to begin at 17:00 hrs on 16 June (D Day + 1) was soon behind schedule as Saito had grossly underestimated the time it would take all the available tanks to move to their attack positions. His intention had been to catch the Marines in the act of digging-in for the night, but the effects of Clausewitzian 'friction' meant that the attack would not go in until the early hours of the following morning. In other words, the law of 'what can go wrong, will go wrong' served to ensure that the attack would be launched not in daylight, but in the dead of night.

It was not until 02:30 hrs that Japanese tank crews finally started their engines. Unfortunately for them, the waiting Marines had heard their engine noises earlier in the day when they were moving into position for the attack. Anticipating the next Japanese move, the Americans brought up the 2nd Marine Tank Battalion which was equipped with the M4A2 Sherman. There were also M3A1 halftrack-mounted 75 mm guns, anti-tank guns, artillery, and bazooka teams on standby, all ready to counter any Japanese thrust towards the beach. The attack was finally launched at 03:30 hrs, over ten hours behind schedule. Sergeant Shiro Shimoda (crewman in a Ha-Go tank) later recalled the opening stages of the attack:

We had to advance in two columns due to the rough terrain. Usually the line formation was used for the attack, but we were forced to advance in a disadvantageous formation. Our tanks rumbled down the ridge and dashed into the enemy positions. Infantrymen rode on the backs of our tanks. 'Fire into the sky', shouted Sergeant Major Nakao, my tank commander. Because of the column formation, shooting forwards would damage a friendly tank; so he told us to fire into the sky to frighten the enemy with our tracers. I aimed my machine gun upwards and pulled the trigger ...

The Japanese tanks advanced in groups of four or five. The ineffective tactics they employed this night reflected the confusing orders issued by Saito. While some tanks made a determined dash for the Marine's positions, others 'cruised about in an aimless fashion.' Several tanks succeeded in piercing the enemy front lines, but the Marines simply shifted their positions to pour concentrated fire on the infantry riding on the tanks. Captain Taisa Shimamura stated after the battle that, 'One battalion broke through a portion of the enemy's line ... but we suffered great losses.'

It was B Company of the 1st Battalion, 6th Marine Regiment, and to a lesser extent, the 1st Platoon of the 2nd Battalion, 2nd Marine Regiment that bore the brunt of the Japanese attack. As such, the destruction of the bulk of the Japanese tank force was largely achieved with 'weapons organic to the infantry battalion.' In many instances, tanks were hit multiple times by Marines from more than one unit. As C. W. Hoffman noted, 'Just how many were knocked out by bazooka men and how many by 37's, 75 mm halftracks and tanks cannot be accurately determined.' Stopping the attack in its tracks was certainly a morale booster for the Marines who were now convinced that they had the right weapons for the job.

In describing the reason for the failure of the attack, Colonel Takuji Suzuki, Chief of Staff of the 43rd Infantry Division, commented that, '... as soon as the night attack units go forward, the enemy points out targets by using the large star shells which practically turn night into day. Thus the manoeuvring of units is extremely difficult.' Burning Japanese tanks also illuminated the battlefield, silhouetting other tanks emerging from the shadows. The fierce battle continued with the carnage on the Japanese side increasing by the minute. From the sidelines, Sergeant Shimoda watched the unfolding chaos. Later he recalled the scene:

There were still tanks running some ten metres from us. The Americans were still destroying our tanks. Sergeant Major Kawakami, my comrade since Manchuria, bailed out of his damaged tank and rushed an enemy position alone, brandishing his sword. I was feeling too self-conscious to remain just an onlooker; sometimes I tried to move forward holding the machine gun, but I was stopped by Sergeant Major Nakao. He said, 'Don't be in a hurry to die—the fight has just begun. Trust me in this matter.' Two hours later we were [still] watching the fight.

As dawn broke, the smouldering hulks of at least 24 Japanese tanks littered the battlefield. Having survived the battle, Shimoda provided a tragic account of its aftermath:

Sergeant Major Nakao ordered us to withdraw to the company HQ at Chacha. While we were crawling up the rocky mountainside trying to find our way back to HQ, Nishida's lone tank passed us, heading to the rear. He stopped the tank at the ridge and shouted, 'All our friends were annihilated.' It was the end of the 9th Tank Regiment.

One of the tanks withdrawing back to Chacha was spotted winding its way up Hill 790. An American destroyer quickly acquired the target and 'fired twenty salvos', destroying the tank which, 'sent up an oily smoke and burned for the rest of the day.' This was indeed the end of the 9th Tank Regiment as an effective force, although the few surviving tanks continued to fight on until ineffective piecemeal attacks on Marine positions on June 23 and June 24 resulted in the almost complete destruction of the regiment.

There are several reasons why the Japanese massed tank attack on Saipan failed. Foremost of these must be the delay in launching the attack which effectively eliminated any possibility of achieving tactical surprise. It could also be argued that launching the attack in daylight would have had a greater psychological effect upon the Marines, as massed Japanese tank attacks were a previously unheard of phenomenon in the Pacific theatre. Difficult terrain also played a part as it forced the advancing tanks to adopt a column formation which greatly reduced their collective firepower. The advance also lacked coordination which to some degree can be explained by the terrain, but was largely due to a lack of clarity in the attack orders issued by Saito. Finally, the steadfastness of the Marines represented a daunting challenge for the Japanese tank crews.

In China, opposing troops had fled at the first sight of tanks because they did not possess the weapons to counter them. On Saipan, the Marine's organic weapons provided sufficient firepower to stop the Japanese attack in its tracks. Confidence in these weapons no doubt bolstered the Marines morale and determination to hold their ground. It was now clear that Japanese tanks needed to be used in a way in which aided the defence most effectively. Massed attacks were clearly not the answer.

11

'The Enemy Must Be Annihilated'
Japanese Armoured Tactics during the Defence of Luzon.

By the late summer of 1944, Japanese losses in raw materials transported by sea had become so great that Tokyo's attention was drawn towards the defence of the Philippines. The loss of these territories would result in the shipping lane to the south being completely cut off, rendering the fleet useless for want of fuel. The Emperor too was concerned about the effect the loss of the Philippines would mean for the Japanese war effort. On 7 September 1944, he argued that the war needed to be prosecuted more vigorously:

> Today our imperial state is indeed challenged to reach powerfully for a decisive victory. You who are leaders of our people must now renew your tenacity and, uniting in your resolve, smash our enemies' evil purposes, thereby furthering forever our imperial destiny.

In spite of the Emperor's fine words, the imperial destiny he spoke of was not to be furthered by the decisive Tsushima style battle conceived by Admiral Soemu Toyoda. In reality, Toyoda's plan was a desperate gamble which would at best buy Japan some more time. But if it failed, it would mean that the defence of the last island outposts was doomed from the start.

On 20 October 1944, General Douglas MacArthur fulfilled his promise to return to the Philippines. On A-Day, four divisions of General Walter Krueger's 6th Army stormed Leyte's beaches at Dulag and Tacloban. They met with little resistance and so were able to quickly establish a firm lodgement. As MacArthur's troops consolidated their positions, the Japanese gamble to score a decisive victory at sea was already under way as two naval task forces steamed towards the Philippines for the showdown which would bring the American advance to a shuddering halt. A surface fleet consisting of the super-battleships *Yamato* and *Musashi*, the battleships *Nagato, Kongo* and

Haruna, eleven heavy cruisers, two light cruisers, and nineteen destroyers under the command of Vice-Admiral Takeo Kurita was heading towards the San Bernardino Strait. His aim was to link up with other surface forces commanded by Vice-Admirals Shoji Nishimura and Kiyohide Shima, and then to use their combined forces to destroy American naval units supporting the landings on Leyte.

Kurita's hopes of making the most of the 'glorious opportunity' presented to him by the Imperial Headquarters in Tokyo were soon dashed when his own flagship, the heavy cruiser *Atago* was sunk by an American submarine. Kurita survived the sinking and transferred his flag to the super-battleship *Yamato.* Six hours later, a message from Combined Fleet confirmed what Kurita already knew, his fleet had been spotted. This alarming message should have been the signal to abandon the operation, but Tokyo confirmed that the operation was to go ahead as planned. Kurita's worst fears were confirmed the following morning when an American search plane picked up his fleet in the Sibuyan Sea. Later that morning, American carrier-borne planes attacked, with the *Musashi* bearing the brunt. After taking more than forty hits by bombs and torpedoes, the great leviathan finally succumbed, turned-turtle, and sank.

In the meantime, Vice-Admiral Jisaburō Ozawa's carrier force consisting of the fleet carrier *Zuikaku,* light carriers *Zuiho, Chitose* and *Chiyoda,* and the hybrid battleship semi-carriers *Ise* and *Hyūga* were experiencing difficulties in fulfilling their role as decoys. Ironically, this was the one Japanese force that wanted to be discovered. It was not until the afternoon of 24 October that the Americans finally picked up Ozawa's carriers. Believing them to be a greater threat than Kurita's surface force, Admiral 'Bull' Halsey headed north on an interception course, leaving the San Bernardino Strait virtually unguarded. Kurita's still powerful surface force was therefore able to steam unopposed off Samar Island where he achieved complete tactical surprise by catching Admiral Clifton Sprague's 'baby flattop' carriers and their weakly-armed escort vessels in the open. Closing in, Kurita radioed Combined Fleet:

BY HEAVEN-SENT OPPORTUNITY, WE ARE DASHING TO ATTACK ENEMY CARRIERS. OUR FIRST OBJECTIVE IS TO DESTROY THE FLIGHT DECKS, THEN THE TASK FORCE.

Minutes later, hot steel began to rain down on the American carriers, not least from the *Yamato's* massive eighteen inch guns. The attack should have spelt disaster for the American Task Unit, but a series of near-suicidal counter-attacks launched by the destroyers *Hoel, Heerman, Johnston,* and *Samuel B. Roberts* saved the day by inflicting heavy damage on Kurita's force. At the same time, the added weight of air attacks launched by Admiral Felix Stump's neighbouring Task Unit served to convince the now wavering Japanese Admiral that he had engaged a major fleet unit. At this point, Kurita decided to disengage, thus throwing away a once in a lifetime opportunity to destroy a detached portion of the American fleet, and the valuable transport and support vessels without which the invasion could not have proceeded.

Time was closing in on Ozawa's carriers, whose mission had been rendered largely redundant by Kurita's failure to realise that the main American carrier force had been lured away as planned. At 08:00 hrs on 26 October, 180 American dive bombers, torpedo planes and fighters attacked Ozawa's carriers. Air strikes continued unabated for several hours during which time the Japanese combat air patrol was totally destroyed. Without air cover, the Japanese carriers were sitting ducks for the experienced American pilots who succeeded in destroying the fleet carrier *Zuikaku,* the light carriers *Chitose* and *Zuiho* and the destroyer *Akizuki.* During the course of the attacks, the light carrier *Chiyoda* and the cruiser *Tama* also suffered heavy damage. Combined Fleet could take no comfort from the pounding given to the American carriers by Kurita's surface force as their plan to destroy invasion shipping had not only failed, it had also resulted in the irreplaceable loss of four carriers, three battleships, six heavy cruisers, three light cruisers and ten destroyers. The disaster at Leyte Gulf signified the end of offensive operations by the Navy. Moreover, as command of the ocean passed to the Allies, any hope of sustaining a prolonged defence of the Philippines was gone.

The crushing naval defeat at Leyte Gulf was not publicised in the Japanese press, nor was news of it passed on to commanders in the field. As such, General Sōsaku Suzuki showed little concern about the future. Indeed, so confident was he of success that he told his Chief of Staff General Yoshiharu Tomochika that, 'We must demand the capitulation of MacArthur's entire forces, those in New Guinea and other places as well as the troops on Leyte.' On 29 October, nine days after American forces had landed on Leyte, General Yamashita's operations officer Major Shigaharu Asaeda flew in from Manila to promise Suzuki a continuous flow of reinforcements. During the course of his visit, Asaeda made no attempt to inform Suzuki about the catastrophic naval battle, but merely contented himself with mouthing encouraging words to stiffen the unsuspecting commander's resolve.

Reinforcements were indeed dispatched to Leyte from Luzon for a decisive showdown with the Americans. These reinforcements included the 1st Infantry Division (two tank companies were attached to the division) which was scheduled to land at Ormoc Bay, situated on Leyte's west coast. At the same time, the 26th Infantry Division was slated to disembark at Carigara in the north. The general plan was for the two forces to combine in order to launch a concentrated attack aimed at retaking Tacloban. As the Japanese attacking force was infantry heavy, tanks were destined to play a minor supporting role in the great victory which Suzuki had prophesied. 'We are about to step on the centre of the stage' said the self-assured commander.

During the initial stage of the invasion, the only Japanese tank unit that had been available was Captain Kawano's 7th Independent Tank Company which was equipped with eleven obsolete Type 89 I-Go medium tanks. Three of these tanks were destroyed around the invasion area at Dulag in a night-attack on D-Day while the remainder were abandoned shortly afterwards. These aged relics of Japan's entry into the modern world of mechanised warfare were soon replaced by more modern tanks as substantial reinforcements began to arrive on Leyte. These reinforcements included the twenty Ha-Go light tanks of the 1st and 2nd Independent Tank Companies and the ten Type 2 Ka-Mi amphibious tanks of the Special Naval Landing Forces. While this fresh injection of armour did not exactly tip the scales in favour of the Japanese, the balance of forces was now a little more even.

Having lost the entirety of the 7th Independent Tank Company in a fruitless assault, the Japanese commanders on Leyte ensured that their tank reinforcements were carefully husbanded. In effect, this meant subordinating them to the infantry in a purely defensive role. The Japanese defences in the Limon area ran along the so-called 'Breakneck Ridge' which served as a protective barrier for Leyte's northern sector and the valuable port facilities at Ormoc. As long as this area could be held, more Japanese troop reinforcements could be brought in to continue to fight. It was therefore inevitable that the battle for this strategically important area would develop into a slugging match that began to resemble the trench stalemate of the Western Front during the First World War. The Tanks of the 1st and 2nd Independent Tank Companies carried out their support role by initially being utilised as prime movers for artillery, then as ammunition carriers, and finally as artillery defending the ridges above the Limon Pass. One by one, Captain Uchida's and Captain Kurobe's tanks were lost, frittered away in piecemeal engagements with an enemy whose strength was growing every day.

By the end of November, the sheer weight of steel thrown by the American artillery began to make holes in the Japanese defences on the ridge. Then, an amphibious landing by American troops south of Ormoc resulted in an envelopment of Japanese defenders which threatened their whole position in the north. On 25 December, Suzuki received orders from General Yamashita to extricate his troops from the ridge and reposition them for a last stand:

REDEPLOY YOUR TROOPS TO FIGHT EXTENDED HOLDING ACTION IN AREAS OF YOUR CHOICE. SELECT AREAS SUCH AS BACALOD ON NEGROS WHICH ARE HIGHLY SUITABLE FOR SELF-SUSTAINING ACTION. THIS MESSAGE RELIEVES YOU OF YOUR ASSIGNED MISSION.

The message also made it clear to Suzuki that there would be no more reinforcements. In spite of this, he clearly understood what was required, in that both he and his garrison would have no other option than to fight on to the death. Despite the bravery of his troops, it made sound tactical sense to immediately authorise the withdrawal from the Limon Pass. The three remaining tanks available to his retreating forces provided valuable cover, but in the process all were destroyed. Their loss was not entirely in vain as more than 10,000 Japanese troops managed to pull back to the rugged Mount Canguipot, a natural fortress located between Palompon and San Isidro on Leyte's west coast. Despite having successfully extricated his troops, Suzuki was experiencing some doubts about the wisdom of holding out, as despite having prepared for a long siege, his troops were beginning to succumb to the ravages of starvation. As time went on, stragglers found their way to the mountain strongpoint, thus compounding his already perilous supply situation. Acting against type, Suzuki faced reality by taking the decision to sanction seaborne evacuations. More than 750 of his troops were evacuated to Cebu in mid-January 1945 before the advance of the American Eight Army cut off the escape route. Officially, the battle for Leyte was over, but resistance in the form of guerrilla actions continued until April.

For Japan, the defeats on land, sea, and in the air during the battle for Leyte were of catastrophic proportions. The disastrous campaign had resulted in the destruction of an entire army, and the permanent crippling of the remaining fleet and airborne assets. Moreover, the tremendous losses sustained had greatly denuded the nation's ability to defend itself against the American naval task forces and bombers. The defeat also raised questions about how to defend Japan's remaining territories from the onslaughts of the American colossus. Analysing the Japanese performance on Leyte, the respected novelist, literary critic and lecturer Ōoka Shōhei (who was himself captured on Leyte on 25 January 1945) considered that the defeat was largely due to a combination of, 'Strategic mistakes', and a 'lack of realistic, practical imagination and enduring fantasies of come-from-behind victory.' Shōhei's remarks about the 'retarded, uncoordinated modernisation' of the Army are also worth noting. At no point during the second phase of the battle for Leyte was any real thought given to the employment of tanks along modern lines.

As late as 1944, many Japanese officers still continued to display many of the traits which reflected 'a distinct yearning for an idealised past'. Perhaps they found this nostalgic reverie both more palatable and easier to comprehend than the more complicated realities of the present day. As a result, few officers came to understand that tanks had become an integral part of modern warfare. And yet, there was one exception to be found amongst these traditionalists, a senior officer whose experience of employing tanks had set him apart from the rest. General Yamashita, the 'Tiger of Malaya' was about to put all of his knowledge and insight to the test in what would be his last battle.

An infantryman at heart, General Yamashita was nonetheless a realist who recognised that tanks would have a role to play in the protracted struggle he had planned for the defence of Luzon. At his disposal, he had the understrength 2nd Tank Division commanded by Lieutenant General Yoshihara Iwanaka. Two tank companies from the division had been transferred to Leyte, while more tanks had been lost when the transports carrying them to Luzon were attacked by submarines. As no further reserves of modern armour were available, Iwanaka had no other alternative than to make use of some obsolete Type 89 I-Go medium tanks left over from the occupation of the Philippines in 1942. These old tanks were subsequently absorbed into the miscellany of tank types making up the 2nd Tank Division. The most effective tank available to Iwanaka was the Shinhoto Chi-Ha medium tank, but these newer models were few in number. The most numerous tank types available for the defence were other older models including Type 97 Chi-Ha medium tanks and Type 95 Ha-Go light tanks. Iwanaka could also call upon 1st Lieutenant Matsumoto's 8th Independent Tank Company equipped with eleven Type 89's, 1st Lieutenant Nakajima's 9th Independent Tank Company equipped with the same number of Type 89's, Captain Iwashita's eponymous tank company equipped with eight improved Type 97's, and Captain Sumi's independent self-propelled gun company equipped with four Type 4 Ho-Ro self-propelled howitzers.

American forces landed along the Gulf of Lingayen on 9 January 1945. The landing was lightly opposed as Japanese opposition on the first day was limited to harassing fire from mortars and artillery directed at the San Fabian beachhead. On D-Day plus one, Japanese tanks from the 7th Tank Regiment ambushed advancing American M4 Shermans on the road to Urdaneta. Two of these tanks were destroyed by flanking fire directed at its weaker side armour. This victory was however short lived as the Shermans following on were able to engage the markedly weaker Japanese tanks which were then destroyed in a piecemeal fashion. Despite the losses incurred by the Japanese, this small-scale tank battle clearly demonstrated that while their tanks were too weak to face the heavier American tanks head on, they could still be effective when deployed imaginatively in well concealed ambush positions or used in creative counterblows.

Not content with simply reacting to American moves, Yamashita planned a more proactive and aggressive strategy based on enveloping the enemy whose advance would inevitably lead to extended lines of communication. With this in mind, he ordered the 2nd Tank Division to move its main body to the line of the Agno River from where he planned to launch his counter-thrust. His ambitious plan certainly had merit, but Filipino guerrilla activity in the rear areas was seriously disrupting the flow of essential supplies to his troops in the Baguio–Mankayan–Bambang Triangle. The threat to Yamashita's supply lines meant that he had no other choice than to choose a more basic plan of attack which involved a limited counterstroke against the American beachhead. His primary objective was to 'effect maximum destruction of enemy weapons, supplies and key base installations' in the San Fabian–Alacan sector. On 14 January, Lieutenant-General Fukutaro Nishiyama, commanding the 23rd Infantry Division, issued orders for the plan of attack. The 58th Independent Mixed Brigade and the 71st and 72nd Infantry Regiments were ordered to hand pick troops for a special raiding party which would be supported by demolition squads. The raiding party was to be further reinforced by a company of mobile infantry drawn from the 23rd Infantry Division and a medium tank company from Major-General Isao Shigemi's 3rd Tank Brigade.

These specially chosen units were tasked with penetrating the American beachhead at different points simultaneously in the early hours of 17 January. After completing their mission, the assigned units were to withdraw. No plan survives first contact with the enemy, and this was certainly the case on this occasion as increased enemy activity meant that the 72nd Infantry Regiment was unable to participate in the attack. The combined tank–infantry forces assigned to the attack also experienced difficulties as a meeting engagement with strong enemy forces west of Binalonan obliged them to withdraw. Despite two of the four units allocated to the mission being effectively *hors de combat,* the mission went ahead. Predictably, this small-scale spoiling attack was a failure. Henceforth, the American build-up continued largely unimpeded.

Following the failure of the Japanese attack, Yamashita wanted to ensure that no more of his precious tanks were needlessly squandered. He therefore ordered the 2nd Tank Division to adopt a defensive posture in positions around Baguio, Lupao, San Ishidro, and San Manuel, northwest of San Jose. Tanks became pillboxes, one Japanese officer remarking that, 'General Yamashita, being an old time infantry soldier, did not believe in mechanised warfare.' This comment was rather unfair as Yamashita had employed tanks imaginatively during his advance down the Malayan Peninsula and during the early stages of the fighting on Luzon. His decision to use them in this way stemmed from rationality rather than an outdated traditionalist outlook. Despite losses, the 2nd Tank Division remained a potent threat, capable of making the American invaders pay in blood for every yard of their advance.

On 22 January, American spearheads clashed with outpost patrols of the Takayama Detachment on the road from Tarlac to Bamban. The following day, elements of the American 37th Infantry Division began probing the Japanese defences to the west of Highway 3. Meanwhile, another probe towards Mabalacat and Angeles forced the Japanese defenders back towards their main positions in the Clark Field–Fort Stotsenburg sector. On 28 January, strong American forces 'wheeling west from Highway 3 launched an attack in force toward Clark Field and Fort Stotsenburg. Japanese armour in this sector consisted of the Iwashita Independent Tank Company equipped with eight Chi-Ha tanks and the Sumi Independent Self-Propelled Gun Company which could field two Ho-Ro self-propelled guns. In a hard-fought action the Japanese tanks claimed one American M7 medium tank and one M18 tank destroyer. Japanese losses amounted to four tanks. The surviving Japanese armour retreated to Mount Pinatubo where a static defence was established. During the ensuing fighting, all of the Japanese armour was destroyed.

The 7th Tank Regiment had been reduced to thirty-four serviceable tanks following the failed attacks at Lingayen and Urdaneta. Unrelenting American pressure forced the regiment to pull back to San Manuel, where the remaining tanks dug in along the fan-shaped road leading to Rosario. The Japanese positions were then subjected to intense attacks from aircraft and artillery which lasted for five days. On the morning of 26 January, approximately fifteen Sherman tanks approached the defence line. Outgunned, the Japanese tanks could make no impression on the Shermans which began to methodically destroy the dug in tanks. By the following evening, only seven Japanese tanks remained. Facing certain annihilation, the 3rd Brigade commander and the 7th Tank Regiment commander led a Banzai charge which led to their deaths and the complete destruction of their units.

On 31 January, elements of the 10th Tank Regiment dug in around Baguio, Lupao, and San Ishidro were attacked by carrier-based aircraft which proceeded to inflict heavy losses. In the meantime, the remaining tanks of the 3rd Company found themselves in an equally precarious position after they were surrounded in Lupao by superior American forces. On 7 February, the company managed to withdraw north-east from Highway 8 to the mountain bastion. Those tanks not destroyed by enemy action were abandoned by their crews during the course of the retreat. The 6th Tank Regiment's positions at Munoz had fared no better, with heavy and sustained enemy fire making their position untenable. Disaster followed the hasty withdrawal of the regiment on the night of 6 February. As the retreating troops headed in the direction of San Jose on Highway 5, 'enemy artillery, antitank guns and automatic weapons raked the column with murderous fire which inflicted heavy casualties and destroyed virtually all tanks, trucks and mechanised artillery.' By the time the regiment reached the relative safety of the mountain near San Jose, it had lost four-fifths of its strength.

The delaying actions fought by elements of the 2nd Tank Division were arguably successful as they slowed down the American advance towards San Jose. Japanese armour also facilitated the withdrawal of the bulk of the 105th Infantry Division to the north together with large quantities of supplies accumulated in the San Jose area. The price however was very high, as only twenty of the 200 tanks fielded by the division on D-Day remained. Significant quantities of mechanised transport and artillery had also been destroyed. The

2nd Tank Division now existed in name only, its few remaining tanks unable to make any impression on the course of the battle.

Yamashita's decision to employ his tanks in a largely static role appeared to contradict Japanese armoured doctrine which viewed the defence as a 'temporary phase of combat', which was only to be accepted when there was overwhelming enemy superiority. The primary object of defensive operations was to inflict heavy losses on the enemy thereby creating suitable conditions to launch counter-attacks. On Luzon, those suitable conditions never materialised as the massive superiority in *materiel* enjoyed by the enemy precluded any real possibility of launching effective counter-invasion operations. Moreover, Army doctrine had always placed infantry units at 'the centrepiece of battlefield operations.' Even as late as 1944, when all the evidence showed that the nature of warfare had changed, field officers continued to cling to the outdated notion that properly led and well-motivated foot soldiers could overcome all obstacles.

During the battles on Luzon, Japanese combat methods continued to display a 'curious mix of backwardness and ingenuity.' Attacks were piecemeal affairs which had a very limited impact on the enemy. The attempt to utilise the 2nd Tank Division in a major counter-offensive came to nothing due to security issues in the rear areas. Following the cancellation of the planned counterblow, Yamashita's decision to fight a grinding war of attrition led to the considerable assets of the division being split up and used to defend key positions. While these tactics may have 'forfeited the principles of manoeuvre and mass used with great success by other combatant nation's armoured formations', they did produce some tangible results. Tanks that had been placed behind earthworks were difficult to detect from the air and also proved less vulnerable to the formidable Shermans.

To a large extent it can be argued that the Japanese Army's continuing inability to innovate was caused by a military culture which discouraged the addressing of those deficiencies which hindered its performance. Yamashita and his staff had no doubt been inculcated with both Japanese doctrine and military culture, but the decision to employ tanks in a static defensive role on Luzon was based not on culture, but on the need to face up to both enemy strengths and Japanese logistical and technical realities.

American intelligence reports continued to state that, 'Defensive combat has been confined to a static defence with a final uncoordinated banzai counter-attack.' These intelligence reports fail to credit Japanese commanders with much creativity or initiative. On Luzon, Yamashita conducted a skilful and well-planned defence using the resources he had at hand. That said; the spirit of bushido was never completely extinguished. As American forces threatened Yamashita's headquarters at Baguio, he ordered the remaining tanks at his disposal to charge a column of Shermans on the road between

Baguio and Sablan. This armoured Banzai attack was however stymied by a lack of resources as the 5th Company of the 10th Tank Regiment could only muster three Chi-Ha tanks and two Ha-Go tanks. Clearly this small force was nowhere near powerful enough to make an impression on the larger and more numerous American tanks. Therefore, a suicide attack was ordered, with two tanks being converted into mobile bombs.

The tactic of using tanks as suicide weapons seemed to confirm the view of American intelligence gatherers. Their inbuilt prejudice did not allow them to see that this episode was not a standard response to an American attack, but one borne out of desperation as the commander's headquarters was in real danger of being overrun. Tu Mu, the Tang Dynasty scholar and commentator on Sun Tzu's *Art of War* said that 'to be on desperate ground is like sitting in a leaking boat or crouching in a burning house.' In other words, desperate situations sometimes require desperate tactics. Therefore the decision to use the few remaining tanks in a suicide mission was a rational one which arguably fitted into the overall defence strategy. For the American command, the failure to comprehend the evolution of Japanese defensive doctrine would have terrible consequences in the months ahead.

12

A Measure of Things to Come
The Integration of Tank Forces into Evolving Japanese Island Defence Tactics

The American plan to invade Guam in June 1944 had been postponed as a consequence of the unexpectedly stubborn Japanese resistance on Saipan and the great naval showdown in the Philippine Sea. On Saipan, the Japanese garrison had conducted a skilful defence which tied up large numbers of American troops for several weeks. At sea, the story was very different as the Japanese Navy was faced with the loss of the three aircraft carriers *Taiho, Shokaku,* and *Hiyo* following a disastrous encounter which had shattered the carefully rebuilt carrier arm. The only glimmer of hope remaining lay in the delay imposed upon American invasion plans which meant that Lieutenant-General Takeshi Takashina and his second in command Lieutenant-General Hideyoshi Obata were given more precious time to prepare their defences.

Japanese garrison forces on Guam included the 29th Infantry Division, the 18th and 38th Infantry Regiments, the 10th and 48th Independent Mixed Brigades, and the 54th Independent Guard Unit. Armoured units on the island consisted of the 1st Company of the 9th Tank Regiment which fielded seventeen Ha-Go tanks, the regiment's 2nd Company which had three Ha-Go tanks, ten Chi-Ha tanks, and one Shinhoto Chi-Ha. In addition, there was the 29th Infantry Division's Tank Unit which could contribute nine Ha-Go tanks to Guam's defence. The area between the capital city of Agana and Agat Bay on the west coast was heavily fortified as the natural barriers protecting the island were less formidable in this sector. Takashina placed eight of his eleven infantry battalions in this area along with the bulk of his tanks which he intended to use as a mobile shock force. His basic strategy adhered to the orthodox doctrinal view which stated that a forward defence was the best means of defeating an amphibious invasion.

Prior to the invasion, the island was subjected to an intense naval bombardment which reduced much of the built-up area to rubble. At 08:29

hrs on 21 July 1944, elements of the 3rd Marine Division began to land on the beach at Asan. After a day of hard fighting, the Marines had established a foothold on the island, albeit with heavy casualties. That night, Takashina launched a series of attacks against the Marine lodgements on the beaches at Asan and Agat. The heaviest attacks were launched against the 1st Marine Brigade in the Agat sector. Five Ha-Go tanks from the 1st Company of the 9th Tank Regiment participated in one of the three attacks. Poor coordination between the Japanese artillery, infantry, and tanks meant that the lightly armed and armoured Ha-Go tanks made little impression on the Marine's defences. Inevitably, a deadly combination of bazooka and tank fire resulted in the destruction of the attacking force. The orthodox approach was clearly not working, and Takashina's blind adherence to outdated methodology was compounded by his badly conceived and organised attacks, all of which achieved nothing. With the senseless frittering away of his precious armoured resources, Takashina had condemned the defence to a grinding battle of attrition which could only have one outcome.

After four days of hard fighting, the Marines succeeded in breaking up the thin crust of the Japanese forward defences and were able to link up their two beachheads. As the 3rd Marine Division headed inland towards the Fonte Plateau, their lines of communication became dangerously overstretched. This opportunity was not lost on Takashina who quickly ordered a general attack to crush his overextended enemy. The 2nd Company of the 9th Tank Regiment was due to take part in the attack, but became disorientated and so failed to reach their assembly point in time. Even without the fourteen tanks that were temporarily *hors de combat,* the night attack launched during the early hours of 26 July still came close to succeeding. On this occasion, the margin between victory and defeat was narrow, but once again the deciding factor was superior American firepower.

On 28 July, Takashina was killed in action during the retreat from Fonte Plateau. General Hideyoshi Obata took over command and set about defending the northern sector of the island with skill and tenacity. The bulk of the remaining tanks at his disposal were used to fight delaying actions which had some effect on slowing down the advance, but the price was heavy as all were destroyed by advancing Marine units. On the night of 5 August, a handful of tanks attacked the positions of the American 305th Regimental Combat Team (RCT) at Pagat. The following day, the RCT came under intense fire from two Japanese tanks as it continued its advance. On 10 August, the last ten operational Japanese tanks were destroyed by Shermans in a vastly unequal contest. After urging his troops to fight to the end, Obata committed ritual suicide.

The initial stages of the bloody defence of Guam were fought with tactics based upon the doctrine of Japanese spirit overcoming all obstacles. When these tactics inevitably failed, the defence began to shift away from costly banzai charges to a more intelligent defence based on delaying actions and ambushes. This evolution in Japanese island defence tactics may have produced greater dividends if valuable troop reserves had not been wasted in the early stages of the battle. Not only troops were wasted, but tanks too, and as a result, the tanks employed in the defence of Guam were only able to make a minor contribution to the island's defence. Badly coordinated attacks launched with insufficient strength achieved nothing, largely because many senior Japanese officers were only just beginning to understand the tactical possibilities that tanks offered.

As the Pacific War entered its terminal phase, Japanese garrison commanders woke up to the new realities facing them and as a result began to utilise more varied and sophisticated tactics. Indeed, Japanese island defence underwent an evolutionary process which to some degree negated America's massive superiority in men and *materiel*. As the Japanese evolved, the Americans stagnated due to the overconfidence that was beginning to undermine the effectiveness of their amphibious operations. General William Rupertus, commander of the 1st Marine Division expressed his abounding faith in the forthcoming attack on Peleliu by stating that, 'it will be a short operation, a hard fought quickie that will last for four days, five days at the most.' His confidence proved infectious, so much so that very few of the thirty-six available accredited war correspondents chose to accompany the invasion force on what was widely considered to be a non-story.

Peleliu's defence was placed in the hands of Colonel Kunio Nakagawa by the commander of the 14th Infantry Division, Lieutenant-General Sadae Inoue. Nakagawa arrived on Peleliu in April 1944. His defensive preparations were based upon the Palau District Group Training for Victory orders which stated:

> ... We must recognise the limits of naval and aerial bombardment. Every soldier and civilian employee will remain unmoved by this, must strengthen his spirits even while advancing by utilising lulls in enemy bombardment and taking advantage of the terrain according to necessity.

Taking advantage of the numerous coral caves and sinkholes in the Umurbrogol Mountains, Nakagawa used his troops and civilian labourers to 'develop natural caves and to construct other emplacements.' Inevitably, his work was to some degree frustrated by inter-service rivalries with the Navy who had considered the Palaus to be their territory. Notwithstanding these difficulties, Nakagawa succeeded in constructing over five-hundred fortified caves and bunkers, based on a 'honeycomb' system in which each strongpoint was connected to another. The defensive preparations on Peleliu included both a forward defence line on the beach and a defence in-depth. These sophisticated defences were an entirely new phenomenon in the Pacific theatre.

To man his defences, Nakagawa had available some 11,000 troops and assorted naval units which he allotted to four defence districts. His defence force was reasonably well-armed, their arsenal including mortars, artillery, anti-aircraft guns, an improvised rocket battery, and the seventeen Ha-Go tanks attached to the 14th Infantry Division. On Peleliu, the defence would be based on rationality rather than the traditional reliance on *Yamato damashii* (Japanese spirit). This meant that there would be no more senseless and costly banzai charges, but a long drawn-out, intelligently constructed battle of attrition which would inflict the maximum number of casualties on the American invaders.

On 12 September 1944, the invasion began as five battleships, four heavy cruisers, and three light cruisers began an intense three-day bombardment of Peleliu. The big guns only paused to allow carrier-based aircraft to pulverise the island's defences with high explosives. After a brief lull, the aerial and naval bombardment was renewed at 05:50 hrs on D-Day (15 September). Bill Tapscott a Marine landing with the 7th Marine Regiment described the scene:

> From all the firepower we were seeing and hearing, we were wondering ... how in the world can anything survive. It was beyond your imagination how anything could be alive, so we were beginning to feel pretty good. By eight o' clock it was fully light. I was watching this one plane ... dropping napalm. All of a sudden it was one big ball of flames ... falling to the ground.

Despite the colossal amount of naval shellfire and aerial bombing unleashed on the island, many defenders survived. As a consequence, the advancing Marines were met with a hail of pre-registered artillery fire which pinned them down on the beaches. Only the 7th Marine Division was able to make some progress in pegging out claims inland. Alarmed at the loss of momentum, General Rupertus hastily threw in his reserves.

The unfolding chaos on the invasion beaches provided Nakagawa with an opportunity to launch a combined infantry-tank attack. At approximately 16:50 hrs, Japanese troops and tanks emerged from the area north of the airfield. The attacking force then swung southwards across the front of the 1st Marine Division's lines. Unfortunately for the Japanese, the attack had been anticipated, and Shermans in defilade positions took a heavy toll on the advancing Japanese Ha-Go tanks. Nonetheless, some tanks managed to break through the American positions, but instead of causing a rout, they became the focus of every anti-tank weapon available. More than100 Japanese tanks were claimed as destroyed, indicating that tanks had been hit multiple times by Marines armed with bazookas, anti-tank gunners and tankers who each thought that they had fired the killing shot. The attack was a dismal failure which failed to dent the beachhead defences.

The Japanese attack was witnessed by Lieutenant-Colonel Robert W. Boyd, commanding the 1st Battalion of the 5th Marine Division. He later recalled seeing, 'Japanese Type 95's ... running around wildly, apparently without coordination, within our lines firing their 37 mm guns with the riders on these tanks yelling and firing rifles.' Another witness to the scene was Lieutenant-Colonel Lewis Walt who noted how the attack was repulsed:

> Four Sherman tanks came onto the field in the 2/5 zone of action in the south end of the airfield and opened fire immediately on the enemy tanks. These four tanks played an important role in stopping the enemy tanks and also stopping the supporting infantry, the majority of which started beating a hasty retreat when these Sherman's came charging down from the south. They fought a running battle and ended up in the midst of the enemy tanks.

Lieutenant-Colonel Arthur J. Stuart elaborated on Walt's description of the attack in an official study into tank doctrine and base defence in which he used Peleliu as an example:

> A Japanese tank company attacked our beachhead at H+6 hours. It was entirely unsupported. This attack succeeded in penetrating our beachhead but did little damage as the Japanese tanks became easy prey to our tanks as a result of the Japanese tank commander's apparent ignorance of the great superiority of our tanks. Nonetheless, this operation is believed significant because (1) the Japanese tanks suffered no damage during the pre-landing bombardment by naval gunfire and air, emerging in full strength to attack after H-hour and (2) the deployed Japanese tank counter-attack successfully penetrated our naval gunfire isolation fires ... Important is the fact that the Japanese tanks were undamaged and that the full complement of the island's tanks penetrated our defence.

The attack failed for several reasons. First, it had been anticipated by the Marines. Second, it was not launched in sufficient strength. Third, the advancing Japanese tanks had left much of their supporting infantry lagging behind.

For both sides, the battle for the island turned into a grinding war of attrition. American superiority in combat power meant that the outcome was never in doubt. This did not mean however that the cost of victory would be cheap. Japanese defenders clung to every rock, every scrape in the ground, and every piece of earth as they attempted to stop the Marines cutting the island in two. The fierce battle for 'Bloody Nose Ridge' inflicted very heavy casualties on Colonel 'Chesty' Puller's 1st Marine Regiment. Having destroyed over 145 Japanese positions the regiment was now at the end of its combat strength. The 321st Regiment of the 81st Infantry Division took over the burden of reducing the remaining Japanese defences. On 24 November, Japanese resistance was finally broken, Nakagawa declaring 'Our sword is broken, and we have run out of spears.' Three days later the island was fully secured by the Americans.

The American casualty rate during the ill-named Operation Stalemate II was the highest of the war to date. The 1st Marine Division alone suffered seventy-per-cent casualties in the seventy-three day battle. Japanese casualties were heavier still with only nineteen soldiers surviving the battle. There is no doubt that this was a clear-cut American victory, albeit won at high cost. That said, the battle failed to conform to American expectations as the Japanese garrison maintained their discipline throughout. There were none of the usual cracks in morale which presaged a senseless mass suicide attack. Instead there was a wholly rational defence strategy based upon mutually supporting, fortified positions which extended into the interior of the island. Tanks had not yet been integrated into this strategy, but the blueprint was now there. What was needed was an officer of moral courage and imagination who was willing to break away from orthodox views. On Iwo Jima there was such an officer.

13

The Sulphur Island
Colonel Nishi's 26th Tank Regiment's Role during the Defence of Iwo Jima

The fierce Japanese resistance encountered on Leyte and Peleliu forced the Americans to delay their invasion of Iwo Jima by two weeks. The delay did not cause any particular concern in Washington as optimistic intelligence reports indicated that the 'Sulphur Island' could be pacified in as little as one week. For ten weeks American bombers flew over the island dropping their explosive cargo. These raids only stopped on 16 February 1945 as it was now time for the surface fleet consisting of six battleships, four heavy cruisers, one light cruiser, and sixteen destroyers to take over. Surely not a living being on the island could have survived?

Despite the blistering bombardment, not all was as it seemed as Japanese troops had dug in deep. These troops were led by Lieutenant-General Tadamichi Kuribayashi who had arrived to take overall charge on the island on 19 June 1944. No fanfare greeted his arrival and almost immediately he came into conflict with Admiral Rinosuke Ichimaru and Major-General Kotau Osugu who both strongly advocated a forward defence on the beaches. These disputes went on for several months and were only partially resolved following a special meeting between senior officers, some of whom had been especially flown in from the mainland.

According to Ensign Satoru Ōmagari who attended the meeting, Commander Kiyoshi Urabe (representing the Third Air Fleet) argued strongly for a waterline strategy by saying that, 'The Navy will transport the necessary supplies for the Army to build 300 blockhouses concentrated on the southern beaches. There is no other place for the enemy to come ashore. We will destroy them as they land.' Lieutenant-Colonel Kaneji Nakane condemned Urabe's statement as nonsense by saying that, 'The Americans have control of the air and the sea, yet the Navy High Command expects us to meet them on the beaches? Have they lost their minds?!' As Ōmagari took notes he noticed that the advocates for a more sophisticated Peleliu style defence in depth all came from the Army. After several hours of heated debate, the meeting adjourned without a consensus having been reached.

Despite the impasse, Kuribayashi remained determined to see that his more forward thinking strategy prevailed. To this end he began to replace those senior officers who continued to resist the idea of a defence-in-depth. Two months after the meeting he replaced the recalcitrant Major-General Makoto Ōsuga with Major-General Sadasue Senda. Colonel Tadashi Takaishi then replaced Colonel Shizuichi Hori as his Chief of Staff. At the same time, two battalion commanders were also replaced. These personnel changes strengthened Kuribayashi's position, but did not give him *carte blanche* to effect his own strategy. Therefore, a compromise needed to be agreed with the IJN. After much haggling, a reciprocal agreement was brokered in which the IJN would transport ammunition, supplies and building materials for inland defences on the understanding that Army personnel would assist in the construction of waterline defences. This compromise may have produced a degree of harmony between the competing services, but in reality it suited neither side as it effectively precluded any possibility of mounting a coordinated defence.

Despite the limitations imposed on him by the compromise with the IJN, Kuribayashi set out preparing the island's defence with a hitherto unknown degree of tactical acumen. To facilitate the construction of defensive positions, the village of Motoyama was dismantled. The reclaimed materials were then put to good use in the construction and furnishing of a maze of connecting tunnels which stretched from the site of the village to Mount Suribachi. More than twenty kilometres of tunnels were completed, although some gaps in the tunnel system between Motoyama and Suribachi remained. Notwithstanding; those sectors that had been fully completed were of a very high standard with, some even having ventilated bunkers which had their own electricity supply. Tunnel entrances were also sharply angled to deflect enemy explosive charges and flamethrowers. As a result of Kuribayashi's indomitable will, Iwo Jima became a killing zone in which there was no dead-ground for the invaders to find cover.

Kuribayashi's basic plan was to husband his forces in carefully laid out positions away from the beaches and then fight a delaying action which would serve to buy time for preparations to be put into place for the defence of the homeland. For the defence of Iwo Jima he was able to call upon the 9th, 10th, 11th, and 12th Independent Anti-Tank Battalions, the 309th, 311th, 312th, and 314th Infantry Battalions, the 5th Anti-Aircraft Unit, the 145th Infantry Regiment, elements of the 2nd Mixed Brigade, the 204th Naval Construction Battalion, the 21st Special Machine Cannon Unit, the 2nd Mixed Brigade Field Hospital, and the 26th Tank Regiment; a total of 22,000 men. These troops were well-armed in that their units boasted a variety of light and heavy weaponry including 361 artillery pieces rated at 75 mm and above, ninety-four dual-purpose anti-aircraft guns, thirty-three naval guns, twelve spigot mortars, sixty-five heavy mortars, 200 light anti-aircraft guns, and sixty-nine anti-tank guns. Tank support consisted of Colonel Takeichi Nishi's 26th Tank Regiment which was equipped with eleven Chi-Ha tanks, some of which were the improved type with the high velocity 47 mm gun, and twelve Ha-Go tanks.

These tanks had replaced the twenty-eight others that were lost after the transport carrying Nishi's regiment was attacked and sunk by an American submarine. It had been necessary for Nishi to return to Japan to collect more tanks. While *en route* to the homeland, he stopped off at Chichi Jima where he spent an evening talking and drinking with Major Yoshitaka Horie. Outlining his situation to Horie, Nishi said, 'I was transferred to the armoured forces from the cavalry and had been expecting to fight in Manchuria or China employing the manoeuvring power and firepower of the tank. Now, instead, I have to go to Iwo Jima. What's more, I have no tanks now. More than twenty of them are at the bottom of the sea.' Horie responded by saying that, 'I understand your situation very well. On Iwo Jima, you probably will have to put your tanks in caves in order to use them as pillboxes. You will not be able to use the manoeuvring power of the tank out in the open.' Nishi was shocked at this revelation, replying, 'In a cave? Can you send a message to the Imperial Japanese Headquarters? If they order us to die, I don't mind dying, but at least allow us to use our tanks in the proper way.' Horie explained that there was no point in pushing the matter further as the policy for island defence had been set. Nishi decided to speak with Kuribayashi on Iwo Jima before heading to Tokyo to collect more tanks. Following his return a month later, defensive preparations had advanced even further. His tanks would have a role to play on Iwo Jima, but not the one he had originally envisaged.

By the end of November 1944, the island was almost ready for the coming battle. Mount Suribachi alone contained more than 100 well-placed artillery pieces. With his preparations almost complete, Kuribayashi wrote to his son Taro and daughter Yoko:

> The enemy landing on my island is merely a question of time. If the defence of this island fails, then Tokyo will be raided day and night … Once Tokyo is raided it means that Iwo Jima has been taken by the enemy. It means your father is dead.

Shortly afterwards he wrote a separate letter addressed to his son in which he expressed his willingness to die for the greater cause:

> I, your father, stand on Iwo Jima, the island which will soon be attacked by the American forces. In other words this island is the gateway to Japan. My

heart is as strong as that of General M. Kusunoke who gave his life for Japan 650 Years ago at the Minato River. As he could not, neither can I expect to return to Japan alive, but I am proud and feel honoured to fight until death comes.

It was now only a matter of time before the invasion came. Consequently, there was no let-up in the construction programme, even though the troops were clearly suffering from the effects of overwork and meagre rations. Ensign Ōmagari wondered to himself, 'What is the point of digging bunkers if we all die before the enemy even lands?'

Following his return to Iwo Jima with the replacement tanks that he had managed to collect, Nishi took the time to write a letter to his wife in which he made no reference to his personal feelings regarding the diversion of his troops or his own transfer to the island:

> The situation on Iwo Jima becomes more serious day by day. We do not know when the enemy will come. If everyone at home is united and works together, I can fight without too much worry. I am confident I can lead the fight here at the head of my officers and men to pay back all the blessings bestowed on me by our country. My mind is as serene as a polished mirror. Remember: help each other and work together.

The situation on Iwo Jima was indeed becoming more serious as each day passed. Men suffering from diarrhoea and dehydration received some relief on 1 February 1945 when an unexpected downpour provided enough water for all of the canteens to be filled.

In their stinking fetid bunkers, Kuribayashi's troops were relatively safe from the incessant aerial bombardments. A handful of Japanese aircraft had responded in kind by attacking American airbases on Saipan, but these raids were mere pinpricks which had little or no effect on their enemy's invasion timetable. On 16 February, Rear-Admiral William H. P. Blandy's Task Force 52 arrived off the coast of Iwo Jima, and following a raid by B-24 bombers, F6F Hellcat and P-38 fighters, the massive naval guns opened fire on the island. Over the next few hours over 200 heavy shells, 6,472 eight-inch, and 15,221 five-inch shells descended on the Japanese positions. As a result of the enemy's very effective radio jamming operations, Japanese messengers were forced to venture above ground as not all the connecting tunnels had been completed.

The naval bombardment recommenced with increased fury on the following day. In spite of this, observations recorded by messengers concerning the condition of the island's defences only served to increase Kuribayashi's confidence that his defences would survive largely intact. Watching the grey leviathans hurling their huge projectiles at the island, seventeen-year-old Radioman Tsuruji Akikusa did not share his commander's conviction. Watching huge chunks of soil and rock being blasted away, Akikusa asked himself, 'Were the Americans trying to wake the volcano by punching a hole in it?' At one point the heavy cruiser *Pensacola* crept to within 1,600 yards of the beach, until a well-placed Japanese 150 mm gun scored multiple hits on the interloper, forcing it to limp away.

Soon after the naval bombardment had lifted, a group of twelve landing craft were observed heading towards the beaches. Japanese heavy guns opened fire, destroying one landing craft and severely damaging another. Assorted small-arms fire then added to the carnage, wounding eighteen crew members on board another landing craft. Kuribayishi believed that he had thwarted the first attempt to invade the island, but this was a pyrrhic victory as the landing craft were not the vanguard of the invasion force, but a support unit assisting frogmen to identify and destroy underwater obstacles. Kuribayashi had made his first, and as it turned out, only mistake. That said, it was to prove a costly one as many of his carefully sighted gun positions had been prematurely exposed. The American response was both swift and violent. A rain of sixteen-inch shells and air-dropped napalm canisters descended on the island. Damage on the ground was difficult to determine, but crucially, Kuribayashi had showed his hand early.

The following morning, the naval bombardment recommenced with renewed ferocity and increased accuracy. Mount Suribachi and Hill 382 received particular attention as heavy shells ploughed-up the island's surface. Five hours later, the bombardment lifted. Sixteen blockhouses, twenty pillboxes, and seventeen shore-batteries, four of which were located at Suribachi's base were destroyed. Despite this pounding, troop casualties were light as the deep caves and tunnels had provided adequate protection. Hunkering down in their positions, the defenders of Iwo Jima began to wonder when the Americans were going to land on the island. They did not have long to wait, as within twenty-four hours they would be subjected to the full fire and fury of the American invasion forces.

On the morning of 19 February, the huge American fleet which had been further augmented with two more battleships, pummelled the island with heavy gunfire for one hour and twenty-three minutes. Then came waves of carrier-borne aircraft which attacked the island's defences with rockets, bombs and napalm. As soon as these aircraft had departed, the bombardment started again, this time with even more fury. The big ships ceased fire at 08:50 hrs in order to give the aircraft another opportunity to strafe the island. Then finally, it was the turn of the rocket ships to drench the island with a fusillade of 20,000 projectiles.

As the rocket bombardment ceased, the first wave of Marines came in to storm the beach at 09:02 hrs. Wave after wave of landing craft then disgorged more men, tanks and other vehicles onto a landing area which was becoming rapidly congested. Observing the scene, Akikusa thought that at this rate the Americans would soon overrun the island. Just then, the Japanese heavy guns and rockets joined in causing carnage on the crowded beach. Akikusa later remarked that, 'The beaches were so full of men, boats and vehicles, that there was no way to miss them. Many were forced back into the water. Yet, I saw many small boats coming and going, bringing even more Marines.' Yet despite the continual reinforcement of the beachhead, progress for the Americans was painfully slow. The expected banzai charge which had characterised so many island battles failed to materialise. General Holland McTyeire Smith, commanding ground operations on the island soon came to the conclusion that the battle was going to be a remorseless battle of attrition, rather than the walkover so many had expected.

Kuribayashi had good cause to be pleased as his strategy was paying handsome dividends. For every one Japanese casualty on D-Day, the Marines had suffered ten. That said, the American invaders had not been thrown back into the sea, and despite their high casualties, some inroads had been made into the Japanese defences. By the end of the first day, the Marines held a line running from the base of Mount Suribachi across the southern perimeter of Chidori Airfield and through to the quarry. This meant that Mount Suribachi was close to being cut off from the rest of the island. Despite this, General Smith was not in a mood for celebrating. Later that day, he told a group a war correspondents that, 'I don't know who he is, but the Japanese General running this show is one smart bastard.' If he had been a fly on the wall, no doubt Kuribayashi would have chuckled on hearing the general's remark.

There was hard fighting throughout the morning of D-Day plus one. The Marines made painfully slow progress, but all that was set to change when Shermans (including flame-throwing variants) joined the fray at around 11:00 hrs. As the battle for Mount Suribachi continued, Lieutenant Genichi Hattori's 10th Independent Anti-Tank Battalion continued to put up extremely fierce resistance. Marine combat teams used flamethrowers, satchel charges and grenades in their grim quest to reach the summit of this important position. Kuribayashi was disappointed that his southern defences had been penetrated so quickly, but was pleased to note that elsewhere, his troops were continuing to inflict heavy casualties on the invaders.

On 23 February, Joe Rosenthal took what is 'arguably the most famous news photo of all time' as a combat patrol planted the Stars and Stripes on the summit of Mount Surabachi. This was a highly symbolic moment, but not by any means the turning point in the battle for the island. The approaches to the north of the island were still covered with formidable defences including pillboxes, bunkers, and dug-in tanks. Against dogged resistance, the American advance slowly moved on, and on 25 February, the No. 2 Airfield was captured after a vicious battle which inflicted heavy casualties on both sides. The following day, three American divisions pushed forward until advance units of the 4th Marine Division encountered the formidable defences of Hill 382.

On the following morning, the attack on Hill 382 developed as Marines backed up by tanks slowly edged forward. The rocky terrain presented problems for the tank crews who had to reconnoitre the ground on foot due to a shortage of engineers. Meanwhile, Japanese tank crews of the 1st Company of the 26th Tank Regiment waited in their concealed positions, poised for action. Nishi had recognised that the topography of Iwo Jima offered very little opportunities for the battle of manoeuvre that he had envisaged. Consequently, he fell into line with Kuribayashi's attrition strategy by either digging his tanks in or carefully placing them in caves.

At close range the 47 mm gun mounted on Nishi's Shinhoto Chi-Ha tanks was capable of destroying a Sherman. During the see-saw battle for Hill 382, eight American Shermans were knocked out and another four damaged by Japanese tank fire. Nishi's tank losses are unknown, but in all probability amounted to the entirety of the 1st Company. Elsewhere, his regiment suffered further losses as the 3rd Company was destroyed defending the No. 2 Airfield. These heavy losses left only the tanks of the 2nd Company available for combat as they had been protected by cave structures.

After ten days of fierce combat on Iwo Jima, American casualties had reached such unprecedented levels that General Marshall's office in Washington had suggested using poison gas to clear the island. Admiral Nimitz considered the pros and cons of such an action, finally rejecting it on the grounds that he did not wish to be the first to violate the Geneva Convention. That left no other recourse than to continue slugging it out against a determined enemy who still controlled more than half of the island.

A Japanese tank attack on the morning of 28 February provided ample evidence that the beleaguered garrison still had plenty of fight left in it. The 21st Marine Regiment responded quickly when the Japanese 2nd Tank Company suddenly appeared in their midst, blasting the Chi-Ha tanks with bazookas. Nonetheless, the attack still made something of an impression on the Marines who must have now been wondering what other surprises lay in store for them. After this brief shock, the capture of the lightly defended No. 3 Airfield and the remains of Motoyama raised the hopes of the advancing American troops. Then, just when it seemed that the worst was over, 'two more heavily defended bastions barring the way to the coast' appeared. The weary Marines were quickly disabused of the feeling that the battle had already been won.

Hill 382 still remained the key to securing the eastern side of the island. Kuribayashi knew this and exhorted his exhausted defenders to keep on fighting. Some of Lieutenant-Colonel Nishi's tank crews answered the call by fighting on as infantry from caves, ambushing Marines and tanks with grenades and mines. On 29 February, American pressure on Hill 382 intensified as over 1,000 gallons of fuel were expended by flamethrower tanks in an attempt to clear out the cave systems. For the cave dwellers east of the hill in the fortified Tamanayama sector, the clank of tank tracks followed by the sudden whoosh and crackle of flame created fear and consternation, Radioman Akikusa recalling that, 'The flamethrower tanks were awful. I heard our troops screaming. The sounds combined to form a buzzing sound like radio static.' For Akikusa and his comrades there was to be no respite and by late evening the Japanese defenders on Hill 382 and those at Tamanayama were close to being totally surrounded. The troops in both positions continued to hold out, but their days were clearly numbered.

On 4 March, Kuribayashi sent a report to the Army Vice Chief of Staff via the radio station on Chichi Jima:

... OUR FORCES ARE MAKING EVERY EFFORT TO ANNIHILATE THE ENEMY. BUT WE HAVE ALREADY LOST MOST GUNS AND TANKS AND TWO-THIRDS OF OFFICERS. WE MAY HAVE SOME DIFFICULTIES IN FUTURE ENGAGEMENTS. SINCE OUR HEADQUARTERS AND COMMUNICATION CENTRE ARE EXPOSED TO THE ENEMY'S FRONT LINE, WE FEAR WE MAY BE CUT OFF FROM TOKYO. OF COURSE, SOME STRONGPOINTS MAY BE ABLE TO FIGHT DELAYING BATTLES FOR SEVERAL MORE DAYS, EVEN IF THE STRONGPOINTS FALL, WE HOPE THE SURVIVORS WILL CONTINUE THE FIGHT TO THE END ...

Two days later, the Japanese defenders of Hill 362C were still fiercely defending their positions. After a series of infantry assaults came up against this brick wall, the decision was made to send in tanks to clear the position. The only Japanese tank available to face this armoured onslaught was the 26th Tank Regiment's last remaining Shinhoto Chi-Ha which had survived the fighting relatively intact. The crew, apart from Second-Lieutenant Michio Otani were all dead. Despite his predicament, this brave young officer decided to stay at his position to confront the American tanks.

Three Shermans headed up Hill 362C, their commanders blissfully unaware that danger lurked ahead. Otani's tank had been cleverly placed in a hull-down ambush position from which at close range he fired his 47 mm gun at the leading tank which came to a halt after being hit. Otani then used his remaining shells to fire at the second tank, but was unable to completely destroy it. Nonetheless, his high velocity tank gun caused sufficient damage to cause the crew to abandon the tank. With his own tank gun now useless for lack of ammunition, Otani ran across to the recently vacated Sherman and occupied the gunner's position. He then fired the Sherman's 75 mm gun, scoring a direct hit on the third enemy tank. His work done, Otani somehow managed to re-join his comrades.

Slowly but surely, the American Marines chewed their way through Kuribayashi's main defences. On 7 March, the 4th Division's 23rd and 24th Marine Regiments battered away at the hilltop strongpoint known as Turkey Knob. This was a hard nut to crack, but elsewhere Japanese resistance on the island was starting to fragment. Some officers decided that it was better to choose the manner of their own death rather than waiting for the inevitability of obliteration or incineration at the hands of the Americans. Major-General Senda signalled Kuribayashi for permission to launch a general attack, in other words a mass suicide charge. Kuribayashi angrily refused, knowing that such futile gestures would only hasten the collapse of resistance on the island.

Senda chose to disregard his commander's instructions and convened a meeting of his officers to discuss arrangements for the attack. Promising to, 'always be at the head of the troops', Senda and his officers sealed the pact with a toast comprised of a single cup of water. That evening, instructions were transmitted by word of mouth to the headquarters of the Naval Garrison troops. Either the message was unclear or it was misinterpreted as it was understood that the attack was to take place that night and not the following day as had been planned. Based on this erroneous information, the attack went ahead as Lieutenant Ōmagari led his men out into the open in order to rendezvous with other units at the Navy Cemetery. Their advance was painfully slow as they crossed unfamiliar crater filled terrain which was frequently illuminated by flares fired by Marines who suspected that something was brewing.

Disorientated and lost, Ōmagari was deciding whether it would be better to return to the bunker when a group of Army soldiers filtered through the area. Not knowing where they were going, Ōmagari nonetheless decided to follow them with his men. More by accident than design, the group eventually reached a cluster of bunkers located in the north-eastern sector of the island which were occupied by the remnants of Nishi's 26th Tank Regiment who were now fighting as infantry. Ōmagari had not received word that the general attack had been cancelled by Kuribayashi and accused Nishi and his officers of shirking their duty. The tolerant and infinitely more sophisticated Nishi replied, 'If one wants to die, he can do it at any time. It is only fifty metres to the American positions.' Unbeknown to Nishi, Major-General Senda was determined to press ahead with the attack.

On 9 March, A patrol from the 3rd Marine Division reached the north-eastern end of the island. That night, Senda carried out his frontal attack. Predictably, the attack failed, with almost every man, including Senda being killed for no appreciable gain. Having missed Senda's invitation for mass suicide, Ōmagari opted to join a tank hunting team. After handing over command of his men to Nishi, he set off into the night. For Ōmagari, officers like Nishi never really understood the complexities of the battle because he conducted operations from his bunker complex. This attack was a classic example of Japanese traditionalism triumphing over common sense, and while Nishi may well have been commanding operations from his bunker complex, he was doing it in a manner which recognised the realities on the ground.

On 16 March, Kuribayashi radioed the Imperial Headquarters in Tokyo in order to transmit what he thought would be his last message. That same day, Nishi and his men attempted to link up with Kuribayashi's headquarters. The 26th Tank Regiment now existed in name only, and while they had played their part in slowing down the Marines, they had no more hope of stopping them than King Canute had in holding back the tide. Indeed, from the moment the first Marines came ashore, the American victory on Iwo Jima was inevitable. Nonetheless, Kuribayashi had achieved what he set out to do. Every day the island held out meant one more day of life for the citizens of the homeland. On 21 March, Nishi was killed, possibly in a firefight near Ginmeisui which was located east of the No. 3 Airfield. Two days later, Kuribayashi radioed Major Yoshitaka Horie on Chichi Jima with a message describing attempts to force his troops to surrender:

ENEMY FRONT LINE 200 OR 300 YARDS AWAY. ATTACKING US WITH TANKS. ADVISED US TO SURRENDER BY LOUD SPEAKER. ONLY LAUGHED AT THIS CHILDISH TRICK ... WE HAVE NOT EATEN OR DRUNK FOR FIVE DAYS. BUT OUR FIGHTING SPIRIT STILL RUNS HIGH. WE ARE GOING TO FIGHT RESOLUTELY TO THE END.

Towards the end, there was nothing left but the will to resist. Three days later, Kuribayashi met his end, either by his own hands or in an orchestrated attack against Motoyama Airfield. To date, it has not been possible to identify his remains.

Kuribayashi had exhorted the High Command in Tokyo to modify future defensive tactics to reflect the recent fighting on Saipan and Iwo Jima. His words though fell on stony ground as they did not carry sufficient weight, largely because he was still regarded as a suspect figure whose sympathies lay elsewhere. The tensions in Kuribayashi's character, along with his reluctance to go to war with America had certainly adversely affected his prospects for promotion, but he accepted the situation with his customary grace. He may have been denied more prestigious posts, but in sending him to Iwo Jima, the High Command had by default picked the right man for the job. Above all, Kuribayashi was a realist who had seen at first hand a 'vigorous and versatile population' at work in Detroit's enormous car plants and the New Jersey shipyards. If anyone understood the Americans, Kuribyayashi did.

Nishi had also been something of an Americanophile, and during his stop off In Chichi Jima, he had spoken about his past with Major Horie, explaining that, 'I know America as a result of my equestrian experiences. I have some friends there too', it is all so ironic.' Having come to terms with the fact that his friends were now enemies, Nishi was more than prepared to do his duty. If he was required to kill Americans, he would have preferred to do so by using his tank unit as a type of 'roving fire brigade' that would be in the thick of the action, moving from sector to sector to focal points of combat. When the realisation dawned on him that Iwo Jima was nothing like China or Manchuria, Nishi reluctantly agreed to sacrifice mobility for the protection provided by tank scrapes, rubble mounds and caves. Adopting static positions greatly increased his tank unit's survival chances. It also opened up possibilities for ambushes in which the less powerful armament mounted on his tanks could be brought to bear at close ranges against the more heavily armoured Shermans.

By February 1945, heavier Japanese tanks such as the Chi-Nu had been produced in significant quantities, but their use had been exclusively reserved for the defence of the homeland. As such, the decision to employ the weaker, more lightly armed and armoured tanks available for Iwo Jima's defence in a static role was the correct one. The Japanese Homeland Defence Strategy outlined in April 1945 served to place tanks within an active defence strategy. This effectively meant that the new tanks which had been developed to take on the American tank forces would not be frittered away on island defence. Okinawa, the last stepping-stone to the homeland would therefore be starved of tanks. Those few available would nonetheless make a significant contribution to the island's defence.

Preparations for the defence of Okinawa began in earnest on 1 April 1944 with the activation of the 32nd Army. Lieutenant-General Mitsuru Ushijima had at his disposal Lieutenant-General Tatsumi Amamiya's veteran 24th Infantry Division, Major-General Keiichi Arikawa's battle hardened 62nd Infantry Division, the 28th Infantry Division, four Independent Mixed Brigades, the Naval Base Force, and the 27th Tank Regiment. In addition to regular units, there was also the 24,000 strong Okinawan Militia, and the 1,780 boys recruited into the Iron and Blood Imperial Corps. The troops on Okinawa were to fight a delaying action for as long as possible in order to buy time for the defence of the homeland, and were to be supported by mass Kamikaze attacks, and the great guns of the super-battleship *Yamato*.

Ushijima wisely chose Shuri Castle as his field headquarters as the ancient bastion had unrestricted views of the island. On the high ground above the cities of Naha and Shuri he oversaw the construction of a sophisticated system of blockhouses, reinforced caves and emplacements, all connected by a network of tunnels. His toughest troops manned these defences, while the less experienced units were stationed in the south where a decoy landing was expected. Ushijima's dispositions were based on his forecast that the main landing would take place at Hagushi Beach on the island's north-eastern coast. If his assumptions proved correct, he then planned to lure the American forces into the interior of the island. Once this had been achieved, he would then tie them down in a protracted battle of attrition. The American carriers would then be called on to give close air support, making them more vulnerable to the proposed mass kamikaze attacks.

A stubborn defence of Okinawa, coupled with the effect of mass Kamikaze strikes was Japan's last hope of forcing the Americans to the conference table. Ushijima had no intention however of replicating Kamikaze tactics on the ground. In no uncertain terms, he told his commanders, 'Do not depend on your spirits overcoming the enemy. Devise combat methods based on mathematical precision; then think about your spirit power.' There would be no useless loss of life on Okinawa as the lessons of Peleliu and Iwo Jima had been well and truly learned.

The landings on Okinawa started on 1 April 1945, in exactly the area predicted by Ushijima. The 1st and 6th Marine Divisions and the 7th and 96th Infantry Divisions met little resistance and quickly consolidated their beachhead. By the end of the first day, the airfields at Kadena and Yontan were both in American hands. Over the next four days the beachhead was expanded further, and by 7 April the Motobu Peninsula had been isolated. On 13 April, the northern tip of Okinawa at Hedo Point was reached by the 2nd Battalion of the 22nd Marine Regiment. Hereafter, the pace slowed down to a crawl as a general advance scheduled for 19 April soon ran into more determined resistance at the Kakazu Ridge. So far, Ushijima's strategy of luring the Americans into a trap was working, but even so, not all of his subordinates were willing to go along with his strategy as their old Samurai spirit was beginning to resurface.

Like many older officers, Ushijima held to the tradition of entrusting operational details to his subordinates. One of those subordinates was the charismatic and slightly unbalanced Lieutenant-General Isamu Chō. Encouraged perhaps by the reports of Kamikaze successes against the American fleet, Chō argued that it was time to go over to the attack. He managed to persuade Ushijima that a night-attack by crack troops would cut communications in the American 10th Army sector, thus opening the way for a large-scale attack. Despite Colonel Hiroshimi Yahara's contention that such an operation would be a fruitless waste of good troops, the attack went ahead. As Yahara had forecast, the attack failed, although some units did manage to reach their objectives, only to be destroyed when the Americans rallied. The failed attack resulted in the loss of the equivalent of four battalions, losses that Ushijima could ill afford.

Meanwhile, the Japanese defenders at Kakazu Ridge continued to hold the line. Colonel Munetatsu Hara's men were protected by an expertly camouflaged network of caves, tunnels and passageways. The intricacy, depth, and sheer number and variety of fortified positions rendered this position all but impregnable. Kakazu Ridge was but one of the many strongpoints on the island, all of which would need to be assaulted in turn by the Americans. For this reason, Ushijima and Yahara had cause to be pleased that Okinawa was still holding out against the vastly superior forces facing them.

One officer who was definitely not pleased with the way things were going was Colonel Chō who had always regarded defensive operations as an anathema. At his insistence, a second conference was held, during which the atmosphere was even more heated than before. This time Chō's arguments prevailed as he succeeded in getting Ushijima to agree to order a general attack which would then develop into the decisive battle for the island. Chō had been backed up strongly by General Takea Fujioka who had been growing increasingly impatient with Ushijima's attrition strategy. The beleaguered commander felt that he had no choice other than to submit to his aggressive subordinates. As before, Colonel Yahara's warnings were ignored by the majority of officers present at the meeting.

As dawn broke on 4 May, the heaviest Japanese artillery bombardment of the campaign was unleashed. The heavy guns were brought out into the open from where they delivered more than 13,000 rounds onto the American lines in support of the attack. In the air, Kamikazes and rocket-propelled MXY-7 Ohka manned-flying-bombs created havoc, sinking seventeen ships and killing or wounding 682 naval personnel. These air attacks continued without let up until 17 May and were arguably the most successful element of the Japanese counter-attack.

The ground attack began on the eastern sector of the front occupied by the 24th Infantry Division. General Tatsumi Amamiya's order to his troops read, 'The division will continue penetration and annihilate him at all points by continuous night and day attacks.' The two pronged attack supported by artillery and tanks would involve the 32nd Infantry Regiment attacking towards the Maeda sector, while the supporting 44th Independent Mixed Brigade swung to the west in order to isolate the American 1st Marine Division. Such was the plan, but almost immediately, Clausewitzian friction in the form of transportation difficulties beset the operation. The hitherto uncommitted 27th Tank Regiment was ordered to move from its position in Yonabaru to support the attack on Maeda.

At the start, good fortune smiled upon the enterprise as the regiment's Ha-Go tanks were able to proceed without incident along the Ginowan Road. Then, their luck ran out when the movement of the armoured column was spotted. Within minutes, American artillery began interdicting the road thus preventing the regiment's Chi-Ha tanks from following on. These tanks were then forced to take a more circuitous route along a roadway which was in such poor condition that wheeled transport and artillery were unable to follow. This road also came under fire from artillery which further compounded the advancing column's misery. One Japanese infantryman later recalled that his unit was shelled all the way to Kochi. The 'terrific bombardment' resulted in many casualties, greatly reducing the unit's combat strength. Only two Chi-Ha tanks were able to reach the jumping-off point for the attack. Later, infantry commanders would complain about a lack of tank support during the operation.

The remnants of the 27th Tank Regiment came under artillery fire again on the road to Ishimmi with several Ha-Go tanks sustaining damage. Regardless of losses, the regiment was still able to put nine tanks into the field in support of a pre-dawn attack against American positions on the eastern end of the Urasoe–Mura Escarpment. American artillery strikes destroyed several more Japanese tanks, after which the infantry first stalled, and then withdrew. Growing impatient with the lack of progress, Colonel Murakami committed his own infantry company. Caught in the open, his troops and remaining tanks were sitting ducks for the American gunners. At 08:00 hrs, the commander of the Japanese 3rd Infantry Battalion radioed the 32nd Infantry Regiment command post at Dakeshi with the message, 'Although the front lines on the high ground southeast of Maeda advanced to the line of the central sector and are holding, further advance is very difficult due to enemy fire. There is no tank cooperation.'

On the evening of 5 May, Ushijima summoned his senior staff officer to discuss the failure of the counter-attack. Not knowing quite what to expect, Yahara's thoughts turned to the future , 'Would he order a final charge? Would this be the end?' Sitting in his usual cross-legged position on the floor, Ushijima began to speak:

Colonel Yahara, as you predicted, this offensive has been a total failure. Your judgement was correct. You must have been frustrated from the start of this battle because I did not use your talents and skill wisely. Now I am determined to stop this offensive. Meaningless suicide is not what I want … Now our main force is largely spent, but some of our fighting strength is left, and we are getting strong support from the islanders. With these we will fight to the southernmost hill, to the last square inch of land, and to the last man. I am ready to fight, but from now on I leave everything up to you. My instructions to you are to do whatever you feel is necessary.

Chastened by the failure of the offensive operation he had so aggressively sponsored, Chō effectively lost all hope and meekly submitted to Yahara's promotion as chief decision maker. The loss of over 5,000 troops, dozens of artillery pieces, and all of the 27th Tank Regiment's light tanks was a serious blow. But even after this semi-disaster, all was not yet lost as the terrain on Okinawa favoured the defence. The numerous fortified ridge lines on the island would serve to slow down the American advance. Bolstered by Yahara's wise counsel, Ushijima now believed that he could still somehow snatch a victory of sorts from the jaws of defeat.

On 13 May, the sector known to the Americans as Conical Hill was captured by elements of the 77th and 96th Infantry Divisions after a fierce battle. This success brought little respite as on the other side of the island the battle for Sugar Loaf Hill was surpassing the battle for the eastern sector in its intensity. The unrelenting pressure exerted by the American forces against the Sugar Loaf Hill fortress finally bore fruit. It was however a bitter fruit, as the cost of victory was 2,662 killed, wounded and missing, including three battalion commanders and eleven company commanders.

The collapse of the Japanese defences at Conical Hill and Sugar Loaf Hill exposed Ushijima's headquarters at Shuri to envelopment, although the area was well defended by troops, 75 mm field guns and dug-in Chi-Ha tanks. In the central sector, the strongly fortified Dakeshi Ridge had fallen, but the defenders of Wana Ridge were still managing to hold on against the heavy attacks mounted by the 1st and 7th Regiments of the 1st Marine Division. While the loss of Dekeshi Ridge troubled Ushijima, he was more concerned about his flanks following the fall of Yonabaru in the west and Naha in the east. Having agreed to the proposal for a withdrawal to the Kiyan Peninsula, Ushijima and his staff began to evacuate the headquarters on 26 May. Rear guard troops slowed down the advance of the 1st Marine Division and the 77th Infantry Division on the Shuri–Wana–Ishimmi area. In the meantime, the main body of troops and the few remaining tanks managed to conduct a skilful retreat towards their final bastion located on the southernmost tip of the island.

On 29 May, the 5th Marine Regiment felt their way towards Shuri Castle Ridge. Meeting little resistance, they swept on to the ruins of the castle and raised the Confederate flag in lieu of an unavailable Stars and Stripes. While the Marines were celebrating their victory, the remnants of the Japanese rear-guard managed to filter through the American lines to join their comrades on the road to the south. Approximately 30,000 troops reached the new defence lines located around the Yaezu and Yoza hills. The loss rate amongst Battalion and Regimental commanders had been low. Therefore it remained possible for the Japanese to conduct orderly operations almost to the end of the campaign. One of those officers was the commander of the 27th Tank Regiment who deployed his remaining tanks for what would be Ushijima's last stand.

On 5 June, the rain which had lashed the island throughout much of May finally stopped, but not before it had done its work, turning the approaches to Ushijima's final redoubt into a morass of mud. By 8 June, the Americans were on the move again as the ground became a little more firm. Over the next few days their attacks against the heavily defended outposts situated on Yuza Hill and Hill 59 made painfully slow progress as the determined defenders clung grimly to every inch of ground. The deeply entrenched Japanese defenders could only be eliminated by the extensive use of flamethrowers.

On 14 June, the virtual collapse of the Yuzu Dake line appeared to signal that the end was fast approaching. The following day, Colonel Yahara received an unexpected visit from the 44th Independent Mixed Brigade's commander, Major Kyoso. This once energetic and vigorous man was now a pale shadow. He spoke in a tone which conveyed the utter pointlessness of further resistance:

> The brigade is finished. Our right flank has collapsed. We can fight no more. I regret to report that unit commanders are crying aloud as they watch their men dying in vain. Whatever we do we cannot stop the enemy. Imperial Headquarters never gave us adequate equipment. Our commanding officers are asking if Japan will follow the fate of Okinawa. Why? Is there no alternative?

Kyoso had a point as there was little defensive capability left to combat the massive superiority in men and *materiel* enjoyed by the Americans. Yahara was also well aware of the reality of the situation. Commenting on the impending defeat of Japanese forces in his memoirs, he wrote, 'Most of our soldiers had only small arms and bamboo spears against millions of shells from the enemy's formidable fleet, planes, and tanks. They never had a chance.' Yet, for all these insights, surrender was out of the question. Japanese notions of honour forbade it.

Japanese spirit kept the fight going for another few pointless days. There was no armoured support as all the remaining Chi-Ha tanks had been destroyed. Ammunition of all types was running dangerously low, and communications with frontline units had all but broken down. Nonetheless, an order drawn up by the Senior Operations Officer Hideo Nagano, and signed by Ushijima was issued to the troops:

> My Beloved Soldiers
>
> You have all fought courageously for nearly three months. You have discharged your duty. Your bravery and loyalty brighten the future. The battlefield is now in such chaos that all communications have ceased. It is impossible for me to command you. Every man in these fortifications will follow his superior officer's orders and fight to the end for the sake of the motherland.
>
> This is my final order
> Farewell

On 21 June, American tanks swarmed into Mabuni and then advanced north-west to outflank the defences at Odo. That evening, a telegram arrived from the Army Chief of Staff and the Minister of war. It read:

> For three months 32nd Army has fought bravely under General Ushijima, a commander with great nobility of character. They killed the enemy commander, General Simon Buckner, and delivered deadly blows against his eight divisions of troops.
>
> Your troops struggled hard, preparing superbly for decisive battle. As the enemy strength increased, your troops—officers and men—responded with vows to destroy that strength.

As dawn broke on the following day, news came from a messenger that the 24th Division headquarters was under heavy attack from three directions. Taking their cue as the last few grains of sand drained from the hourglass, Ushijima and Chō committed suicide.

The attritional strategy devised by Yahara and finally adopted by Ushijima had turned the island into a vast killing field of 'mud, decay, and maggots.' Following the failure of the counter-attack on 4 May, this was the only sensible strategy left. Nevertheless, the question still remains as to whether a second Verdun could have been avoided by better tank-infantry cooperation in the early stages of the battle. There is no doubt that better cooperation would have improved the prospects for the success of the May counter-attack. The partial breakthrough by Japanese tanks to the far side of the Maeda Heights was not fully exploited as the infantry had failed to keep pace with the advance, and the subsequent order for the tanks to withdraw to their original start positions was perhaps somewhat premature. After sustaining losses, the regiment's remaining tanks had nonetheless 'achieved an advantageous position.' From here, the counter-attack could have been pressed on to produce the desired 'tipping point' against an enemy who constantly underestimated them. Doubtless the tanks would have been lost in the battle, but in a culture inured to losses, their psychological impact on an overconfident enemy may well have been a price worth paying. Therefore, it could be argued that a more flexible and mobile approach based upon communication and integration may have paid dividends which would in turn have negated the need to adopt attrition as a strategy.

On Iwo Jima, the limited size of the battlefield and difficult terrain dictated the decision to use tanks in a static role rather than as a 'roving fire brigade.' On Okinawa there was ample room for tactical manoeuvre which opened up the possibility of using armour in imaginative ways. This opportunity was however missed, largely as a consequence of the unresolved problem of marrying traditionalism with modern technology. Few senior officers understood how to integrate tanks into a force structure that remained infantry heavy. Of course, to some degree Ushijima's options were limited by the number of tanks available and their quality.

For the defence of the homeland, some possibilities still existed for the imaginative use of armour. Moreover, for the first time, Japanese forces were in possession of a new tank which was a match for the Sherman. The Chi-Nu medium tank had rolled off the production lines in 'significant' numbers, though it has to be said that overall production figures were pitifully small when compared to the output of the American factories. Even so, enough examples of this new tank had been produced for it to play a role in the planned decisive battle for the home islands. This last battle was to be a fully coordinated effort involving all branches of the armed forces and the civilian population. If one hundred million were to die proudly, they would first make the enemy pay a very high price.

Whereas the island struggles were battles in which flesh was pitted against iron, the battle for the homeland would be one supported by hitherto unknown numbers of aircraft and tanks. As intelligence regarding Japanese defence plans filtered through to Washington, the political and military leadership considered the costs for their planned invasion of Imperial Japan. The more they looked, the more daunting the prospect became.

14

Shattered Jade
Japanese Tank Forces and the Homeland Defence Strategy

On 9 March 1945, 325 B-29 bombers set off from their bases on Saipan and Guam to bomb Tokyo. The plan devised by General Curtis LeMay was to drop 2,000 tons of incendiaries on the Asakusa, Fukajawa and Honjo districts which contained a number of factories and worker's housing. In a calculated move, his aircraft would be stripped of their defensive armament in order to increase their bomb load. Furthermore, they would be required to execute the raid at low altitude. Not surprisingly, this revolutionary strategy horrified some of LeMay's flight commanders as they anticipated high levels of crew casualties. Their concerns were not altogether unwarranted as these new tactics certainly involved an element of risk. For the commander of the 11th Bomber Command, the planned raid was also not without personal risk. If his informed gamble went wrong he knew that he would suffer public disgrace at the hands of the press.

The target for the first wave of bombers included the port and docks area. The M-69 incendiary bomblets and M-47 incendiaries dropped by this wave started a series of fires which quickly coalesced into a conflagration of epic proportions. Within thirty minutes Tokyo was burning and the understrength and under-equipped fire services could do little to quell the flames which leapt from building to building. Temperatures reached more than 500 degrees Celsius, the rising heat was so intense that it buffeted the B-29s as they flew across the city. Aircraft from the second wave could not locate their target areas and so simply dumped their bomb loads into the fires. Circling above Tokyo, LeMay's Chief of Staff photographed the devastation. Later examination of the images revealed that just under sixteen square miles of the city had been burned out.

The death toll for this one raid was estimated at a staggering 100,000. Many victims were either suffocated by the intense heat or charred beyond recognition. Those fortunate to survive picked themselves up and went about their business knowing that there was no defence against the military might which America could now project at will across their homeland. On 18 March, the Emperor himself visited some of the bombed-out areas. His aide Kaizo Yoshihashi recorded his observations of the visit:

> The victims were digging through the rubble with empty expressions on their faces that became reproachful as the imperial motorcade went by. Although we did not make the usual prior announcement, I felt that they should have known that this was a blessed visitation just the same, for after all, three to four automobiles bearing the chrysanthemum crest were passing. Were they resentful of the Emperor because they had lost their relatives, their houses and belongings? Or were they in a sense of utter exhaustion and bewilderment. I sympathised with how his majesty must have felt upon approaching these unfortunate victims.

These crass comments serve to demonstrate how out of touch some members of the royal household were. Equally out of touch was former Foreign Minister Kujuro Shidehara who advised the current incumbent Mamoru Shigemitsu that people would soon grow accustomed to the bombings. On 20 May he wrote to his close friend Komatsuchi Odaira stating his firm belief that Japan had to play for time, even if that meant the deaths of thousands of non-combatants. There were many in the military who thought the same way. Even the formal capitulation of Nazi Germany on 8 May failed to change the minds of these hardliners who were increasingly at odds with military and political realities.

On 22 June, the Emperor summoned the Supreme Council for the Direction of the War to his underground bunker in the grounds of the imperial palace. Hirohito was regarded as a living god, but in reality he held little real power on earth. Nonetheless, he was respected as a man of reason, and his sage advice was taken seriously by the seasoned politicians and military chiefs who made up the council. Two hardliners, General Yoshijirō Umezu and Admiral Soemu Toyoda had not been informed about what the Emperor was going to say. As might be expected, their reaction to the Emperor's call for peace negotiations was fierce. Their opposition was duly noted, but they were overruled. They need not have been worried, as in the event, the peace moves suggested by the Emperor amounted to no more than some half-hearted attempts at arranging talks through various intermediaries. As these superficial attempts at peacemaking were being played out, the militarists completed their plans for the suicidal defence of the homeland.

The Imperial General Staff's operational plan represented a deviation from the strategy employed in the recent battles on Iwo Jima and Okinawa. Instead of mounting a defence in depth, the invaders would be met on the beaches with every weapon available in the Japanese arsenal. The intention was not to defeat the Americans, but to inflict such massive casualties upon them that they would accept terms more advantageous to Japan. The whole country would be mobilised to provide the massive forces required to fight this decisive battle with the invader. The basic strategy was to use mass Kamikaze strikes to destroy the invasion force at sea. If enemy forces succeeded in landing, they would be met on the beach by overwhelming force and annihilated.

An analysis of American amphibious operations was used to identify the island of Kyushu as the primary target for the invasion. Consequently, the Japanese High Command allocated the bulk of their remaining resources to this area. The operational preparations were to be conducted in three phases, but only the first phase which involved defensive preparations and troop unit organisation was ever completed. Despite this, morale remained high, one staff officer boasted that:

> We will prepare 10,000 planes to meet the landing of the enemy. We will mobilise every aircraft possible, both training and 'special attack' planes. We will smash one third of the enemy's war potential with this air force at sea. Another third will also be smashed at sea by our warships, human torpedoes and other special weapons. Furthermore, when the enemy actually lands, if we are ready to sacrifice a million men we will be able to inflict an equal number of casualties upon them. If the enemy loses a million men, then the public opinion in America will become inclined towards peace, and Japan will be able to gain peace with comparatively advantageous conditions.

This statement encapsulates the locus of Japanese strategy in the summer of 1945. It was known that the American public had been averse to high casualties since the campaigns on Guadalcanal and Tarawa. Therefore, it was thought that if enough Americans were killed during the invasion, the people would demand an end to the war. There is something to be said about this theory as the 1940s was an information age in which newspapers, radio, and the cinema played a big part in people's lives. Had the news been relayed visually in real time as it was during the Vietnam War, then the strategy devised in Tokyo may well have paid off.

Such was the theory, but in reality, the Japanese Navy had been a spent force since the crushing defeat at Leyte Gulf in October 1944. There were some fleet submarines left, but the main naval effort would be made by manned-suicide torpedoes, midget submarines, suicide attack-boats and frogmen who would release anchored mines in the path of enemy vessels. In the air, great hopes rested on the massed Kamikazes which had inflicted so much damage on the American invasion fleet off the coast of Okinawa. Enough fuel had been reserved to launch waves of 300–400 suicide planes at a rate of one per hour. Approximately 8,000 pilots were available for these operations, but most of them were inadequately trained and would have been no match for the battle-hardened American pilots. Be that as it may, they possessed just enough skill to carry out their suicide attacks against the invasion fleet's carriers and transports.

Ground operations against American landings called for the rapid mobilisation and concentration of forces in the invasion area. For the defence of northern Kyushu, the 56th Army that had been activated on 21 April 1945 based itself around the city of Iizuka which sat at the confluence of the Homami and Onga rivers. Commanding this newly activated force was Lieutenant-General Ichiro Shichida who had at his disposal the 57th, 145th, 312th, and 351st Infantry Divisions, the 124th Independent Mixed Brigade, the 4th Tank Brigade, and the 46th Tank Regiment. For the defence of the southern sector, Lieutenant-General Kanji Nishihara's 57th Army could field the 25th, 86th, 154th, and 212th Infantry Divisions, the 98th and 109th Independent Mixed Brigades, and the 5th and 6th Tank Brigades.

The two tank brigades assigned to 57th Army were almost up to strength. The 5th Tank Brigade could even boast of a partial issue of the new Chi-Nu medium tank within its compliment of fifty-six mediums. In addition, the brigade could also put into the field twenty-six Ha-Go tanks and twenty-four Ho-Ni gun tanks. Training for the tank crews was carried out within the given limitations imposed by the critical fuel situation. But fuel was not the only commodity in short supply, as ammunition stocks were also limited, particularly armour-piercing ammunition for the 47 mm tank guns. The 6th Tank Brigade posed less of a threat to the invaders as it had been denuded following the transfer of its 37th Regiment to Lieutenant-General Mitsuo Nakasawa's understrength 40th Army in Kyushu's southern Satsuma Peninsula. Nonetheless, this was still a force which the American planners could not ignore.

With substantial tank forces available to resist the invasion, considerable work had been carried out towards improving the road network to facilitate counter-attacks. Despite these major road improvements, the movement of some units would have been hampered by a chronic lack of transport, particularly heavy lorries and horses. As a consequence of these shortages, the movement of supplies would have placed an additional burden on the railway system and on rivers and canals, both of which were vulnerable to attack from the air. Not all of the available tanks would have required transportation to the invasion areas as some had been delegated to defend focal points. For example, in the 57th Army sector, the 37th Tank Regiment was placed on standby to counter an anticipated airborne landing.

The general defence plan was to counter the landings at the earliest possible opportunity. If the preliminary aerial and naval bombardment indicated an invasion of southern Kyushu, the 57th Infantry Division, the 4th Independent Tank Brigade, and the Chikugo and Higo Forces would quickly deploy to the Kirishima area in order to repel the invaders. Ground force commanders were instructed to be ready to move troops, tanks, artillery and necessary supplies to threatened sectors at any time. The high degree of flexibility required was not something which had previously characterised Japanese operations, and as such it should be pointed out that the defending troops faced 'distinct limitations in their capacity to conduct protracted battle.' Tactical flexibility was a luxury the Japanese could ill afford. Therefore it could be argued that a defence in depth such as that conducted on Okinawa would have been a more realistic policy.

Preparations for the defence of the homeland were still taking place when the Allies met at Potsdam to determine the shape of the post-war world. There were two major outcomes from the meetings of the so-called Big Three. The first was the Potsdam Agreement which focused largely on German war reparations, the prosecution of war criminals and future land boundaries. The second was the Potsdam Declaration which promised the Japanese complete and utter devastation unless they promptly surrendered. The declaration made no reference to the position of the Emperor, simply stating that, 'The authority and influence of those who have deceived and misled the people of Japan into embarking on world conquest must be eliminated for all time.'

Japanese monitors picked up a broadcast of the declaration on 27 July, the day after it was issued. The ambiguities concerning the Emperor left the government wondering if he would be tried as a war criminal. Kantaro Suzuki, the aged and sagacious prime minister took the view that the declaration had to be treated prudently with a policy known in Japan as *mokusatsu*, which basically amounted to no more than buying time with official silence. In Washington, President Truman failed to understand the cultural basis of Suzuki's policy, seeing it instead as an outright rejection of the declaration. Following discussions with the Committee of Three made up of the Secretary of War Henry Stimson, the Secretary of State Joseph Grew, and the Secretary of the Navy James Forestal, Truman decided to proceed with the plan to use atomic weapons against Japan. The decision to use the bomb was influenced by the apparent Japanese rejection of the Potsdam Declaration and an appreciation by the Joint Chiefs of Staff which estimated that the invasion of Kyushu, first of the home islands, would result in excess of 250,000 American casualties.

On 5 August 1945, technicians at the Tinian air base began the delicate process of readying the atomic bomb known as 'Little boy.' Hiroshima was chosen as a target for the world's first atomic bombing mission largely because the undamaged city served as a military area in which the headquarters of the Second General Army was housed. The city's 'virgin' state also provided an excellent opportunity for scientific observers to note the effects of the bombing. Weather remained the only obstacle to carrying out the mission, but on the following day, meteorologists based at Tinian predicted that there would be clear visibility over the target.

On the morning of 6 August 1945, people in the port city of Hiroshima went about their daily business, oblivious to the approaching cataclysm. As the B-29 bomber named *Enola Gay* arrived over the target, visibility was clear. The bomb was released at 08:15 hrs and took forty-three seconds to reach its predetermined detonation altitude of 1,968 feet. It then exploded with a blinding flash above the Aioi Bridge, instantly vaporising the thousands of people who were within close proximity of the blast area. Despite the devastation caused by the bomb, hardliners such as War Minister Korechicka Anami remained sceptical, stating that, 'We do not yet know if the bomb was atomic.' In the meantime the quest was on to determine the cause of the devastation. Within days of the bombing, Japan's leading nuclear scientist Dr Yoshio Nishina had confirmed that Hiroshima had been destroyed by a single atomic weapon. This news led to increased efforts by the Foreign Office to secure a peace deal mediated by the Soviet Union.

On the afternoon of 8 August, Natotake Sato, the Japanese Ambassador to the Soviet Union requested an urgent meeting with Vyacheslav Molotov, the inscrutable and impenetrable Soviet Minister of Foreign Affairs. Molotov had been avoiding contact with Sato for several weeks. Then out of the blue, he chose to grant an immediate audience. Sato's sense of foreboding regarding this unexpected meeting was soon realised when Molotov presented him with a declaration of war. Little did Sato know it, but Stalin had agreed to enter the war against Japan three months after the defeat of Nazi Germany. Even before the defeat of Hitler's gangster regime had been completed, Marshal Aleksandr Mikhaylovich Vasilevsky had been assembling troops and armour along the Manchurian border. The last great campaign of the Second World War was about to begin.

Following the Soviet declaration of war, Prime Minister Suzuki asked Sumihisa Ikeda, an official recently returned from Manchuria if the Kwantung Army was capable of repulsing Soviet attack. Ikeda's reply was damning, 'The Kwantung Army is hopeless' he said. Meanwhile, Korechika Anami, the unyielding Army Minister took a more sanguine view of the situation, calmly stating that, 'The inevitable has come.' Anami's opinion was shared by the Vice Chief of the General Staff Torashiro Kawabe who rejected previous notions that Soviet neutrality was an essential precondition for continuing the war. There can be little doubt that his thinking was influenced by current estimates of Soviet strength on the Manchurian border. Clearly he was unaware that these estimates had singularly failed to take into account the transfer of massive Soviet reinforcements across the Trans-Siberian Railway. The result of this intelligence failure was that neither he, nor anybody else in Tokyo or Manchuria had the slightest inkling of the true scale of the enemy forces now lining up for the final showdown. The Soviet forces were indeed massive, amounting as they did to some 1,577,725 troops assigned to the Transbaikal Front, the 1st Far East Front and the 2nd Far East Front. These troops were supported by 27,086 artillery pieces, 5,556 tanks and self-propelled guns of modern design and 3,721 aircraft. The Kwantung Army was doomed even before the battle had begun.

The Kwantung Army had long been a symbol of Japanese national pride, but by 1945 this once proud formation was a shadow of its former self as its best units had been transferred either to the Pacific or to Japan for homeland defence. On paper, the 713,720 troops who were backed by 5,360 artillery pieces and 1,155 tanks presented as a powerful military formation. In reality, this was a hollow force largely comprised of partially trained conscripts lacking in experience, tactical skill, and the necessary equipment to confront a superbly trained and equipped foe. In March 1945, the 1st Tank Division (activated at Ningan, Manchuria in June 1942) was transferred to Japan. This left only the inexperienced 1st and 9th Tank Brigades based at Mukden and Ssopingchieh, the 34th Tank Regiment based at Mukden, the 35th Tank regiment based at Changchun, and the 51st and 52nd Tank Regiments based at Siping. When compared to the modern T34-85 tanks and SU-100 tank destroyers fielded by the Red Army, the I-Go, Ha-Go and Chi-Ha tanks which equipped the Japanese tank forces in Manchuria were no more than antiques.

The Japanese High Command was well aware of the Kwantung Army's deficiencies and accordingly ordered it to adopt the age old strategy of the *Cunctator,* first successfully applied by General Quintus Fabius Maximus Verrucosus during the Second Punic War. This strategy was based upon only accepting small engagements on favourable ground rather than risking the entire army in a direct confrontation with a superior enemy. This change in thinking failed to anticipate the high levels of operational and tactical mobility that the Red Army was now capable of achieving. It also failed to appreciate that the Kwantung Army was an infantry-heavy force which lacked the means to outmanoeuvre the highly mobile Soviet armoured forces.

At one minute past midnight on 9 August, the Soviet juggernaut advanced on three fronts against the greatly denuded Kwantung Army that was operating at less than a third of its normal combat efficiency. Following a drive onto the central Manchurian plain, Soviet mechanised forces carried out a classic double pincer movement which achieved complete tactical surprise. The Japanese defenders fought with their usual fanaticism, but could not stop the vastly superior Soviet forces which had developed mobile warfare into a fine art during the long struggle against Nazi Germany. Japanese mobile forces in the form of the tank brigades and regiments had largely been held back and as such there was very little tank versus tank combat during the campaign.

The Soviet broadcast announcing their declaration of war was picked up by the Japanese just before dawn. Neither the monitors listening in or the High Command could have known that this day would also be recorded in history for another notable event, the second atomic bombing. The Japanese may have been oblivious to the second atomic catastrophe about to befall them, but the Americans were experiencing problems of their own as the bombing mission was not going as smoothly as the one carried out over Hiroshima three days earlier. On the morning of the mission, it was discovered that the designated bombing aircraft named *Bockscar* had fuel-pump problems which would significantly reduce its operational range. The scientists on Tinian were already feeling anxious as only the day before three B-29s had crashed on take-off. As one of these scientists later said, 'We all aged ten years until the plane cleared the island'. His worries were more than justified as the lumbering aircraft struggled to clear the runway. Finally, the pilot Major Chuck Sweeney managed to get the heavily-burdened aircraft airborne. At 08.09 hrs, *Bockscar* reached its rendezvous point above the island of Yakushima. Three minutes later *The Great Artiste* which was fitted with instruments for measuring the effectiveness of the bomb, 'loomed out of the clouds'. The third B-29 named *The Big Stink* failed to rendezvous on time and Sweeney used up precious fuel circling for forty-five minutes in the vain hope that the camera carrying aircraft would appear.

As John Toland noted in his excellent book *Rising Sun*, 'The mission was jinxed from the start'. Indeed, nothing seemed to go right as when Sweeney arrived over the city of Kokura at 10.45 hrs, the target area was 'obscured by heavy ground haze and smoke'. After making three attempts to drop the bomb visually, Sweeney turned to Commander Frederick Ashworth, the man in charge of the 'Fat Man' bomb and said, 'We'll go on to secondary target, if you agree'. Ashworth nodded his agreement and *Bockscar* turned southwest towards Nagasaki. Bad luck continued to bedevil Sweeney's crew as the weather conditions over the target were much worse than had been expected. Just when it appeared that the only option left would be to dump the bomb in the sea, a break in the cloud cover appeared over a stadium on the banks of the Urakami River. At 11.01 hrs, *Bockscar* 'lurched upwards' as the bomb was dropped. As a giant ball of flame was seen to erupt over the city, the rear gunner shouted, 'Major, let's get the hell out of here!'

Just as Captain Kermit Beahan was exhorting Sweeney to depart the scene of devastation, an emergency meeting of Japan's Big Six was being convened in Tokyo to discuss the ramifications of the Soviet declaration of war. The meeting had hardly got under way when an officer entered the room to inform those present of the second atomic bombing and the rapidly unfolding calamity in Manchuria. Arguably, the Soviet invasion had shaken the military leadership more than the atomic bombings. This is hardly surprising as conventional land battles they could understand, theoretical physics they could not. Consequently their thoughts turned to Manchuria where the Kwantung Army was being annihilated.

The relentless Soviet advance into Manchuria continued against weak opposition. On 12 August, the Japanese were in a position to put up more determined resistance following the formation of a scratch company consisting of nine Ha-Go tanks commanded by Lieutenant Mizutani which deployed to Aihe, near Mudanjiang. The following day, approximately 100 Soviet T-34 tanks and infantry attacked the Japanese positions at Aihe. Mizuntani engaged the Soviet tanks, but his puny 37 mm guns failed to make any impression on the more heavily armoured T-34s. The Soviet tanks responded, and in short order succeeded in knocking out three of the ludicrously flimsy Japanese tanks. The remains of Mizuntani's company retreated towards Handaohetsi, west of Mudanjiang. At the time of the surrender only three of the scratch company's tanks remained.

Thanks to well organised logistics, the pace of the Soviet advance never slackened, and within the space of one week the campaign had been effectively won. On 15 August, Japan officially announced its surrender to the Allies. Due to poor communications, it took another four days for the order to lay down arms to reach the Kwantung Army. By this time, the Soviet forces had secured all of their objectives. During the course of the campaign Vasilevsky's forces had swept all before them, killing 21,389 troops according to Japanese sources, and 83,737 according to Soviet sources. Some 594,000 Japanese troops were taken prisoner, and many of these unfortunates were to languish in Siberian prison camps until 1949. Along with the defeated Japanese troops, large quantities of arms and equipment were also captured, including 395 Japanese tanks and thirty-five armoured cars. Today, some of these spoils of war can still be seen at the excellent Kubinka Tank Museum near Moscow.

Japanese resistance in Manchuria collapsed quickly due to intelligence failures, communications problems, transportation difficulties, supply problems, inexperienced troop replacements, and weak air support. Armoured support was available, but very few tanks saw combat as the main body of the two tank brigades and four tank regiments were too far away from the action on a line which Soviet forces had yet to reach by the time of the surrender. The speed and relentless drive of the Soviet armoured thrust caught the Japanese command off balance, so much so that they were unable to react quickly enough to bring their own armoured forces into play. The significant number of Japanese tanks and armoured cars in Manchuria must also be weighed against their obsolescence when compared to the modern models fielded by the Red Army. Clearly the lessons of Nomonhan had not been learned as the only modern tank possessed by the Japanese in any significant quantity was not available to the Kwantung Army. That said, it is highly doubtful that if even if the entire production of the Chi-Nu had been diverted to Manchuria they would have made much difference. In 1945, the Red Army's armoured forces had both quality and quantity.

At noon on 15 August 1945, radio announcer Chokugen Wada spoke to the Japanese people, 'This will be a broadcast of the gravest importance. Will all listeners please rise, His Majesty the Emperor will now read his imperial rescript to the People of Japan. We respectfully transmit his voice.' There was a pause while the national anthem was played, then a voice which few had ever heard before crackled on the airwaves. In this unprecedented royal address, the Emperor spoke in a courtly language peppered with classical phrases. Despite this, most people understood his meaning when he said that the war was over and that for the first time in 2,000 years Japan had to submit to the will of a conqueror.

On Shumshu Island, located in the distant Kuril Islands Chain, the Japanese garrison of 8,000 troops which included the crews of the 11th Tank Regiment received the news with the same degree of shock and bewilderment as those in the homeland. The garrison was ordered to prepare for disarmament, and to this end, Colonel Sueo Ikeda's tank crews ceased maintenance and began the process of removing guns and ammunition. The garrison's position was though somewhat ambiguous as the Japanese government reserved the right for the troops on Shumshu to defend themselves in the event of Soviet aggression. Stalin's territorial ambitions were such that an attack on the island was inevitable. He could have negotiated for control of the island as part of the post-war settlement. However, spilling Soviet blood to gain control of this strategically important outpost gave him a moral claim which the Americans would find hard to refuse.

On 18 August, 8,360 Soviet troops stormed ashore. The landings did not go particularly smoothly as nineteen out of twenty radio sets were damaged by seawater. Neither did the assaulting troops expect to meet the fierce resistance mounted by the Japanese 91st Infantry Division. At their base at Shikondai, the 11th Tank Regiment began to frantically reverse the process of disarmament started a few days earlier. Crews continued to work on their tanks even as they were moving from their south-western base to the island's interior at Mount Tenjin. By early evening, approximately thirty of these tanks had advanced as far as Mount Shirei. At 18:50 hrs, the tanks engaged a Soviet infantry company and quickly overran them. Colonel Ikeda then decided to advance towards the landing area to engage Soviet forces there. Ikeda's tanks scattered Soviet troops like ninepins as they crashed into their beach positions. As fog began to descend on the battlefield, a wild and confused firefight ensued as neither the attacking tanks or the hastily unloaded Soviet anti-tank guns were able to locate their targets. In the melee approximately 100 soviet troops were killed. The Japanese had gambled that their tanks could provide a decisive victory. On Shumshu, that gamble almost paid off.

Japanese losses on Shumushu amounted to ninety-six killed, including Ikeda and four of his company commanders. Twenty-one Japanese tanks were destroyed in this engagement, notable for being the last armed confrontation of the Second World War. On 20 August, Soviet and Japanese forces on the island concluded a formal cease-fire agreement, following which came the formal surrender of all defending forces on the island.

Epilogue

Following Japan's decision to surrender to the Allies, a formal end to hostilities took place on board the American battleship USS *Missouri* on 2 September 1945. At 09:04 hrs, Foreign Minister Mamoru Shigemitsu stepped forward to sign the instrument of surrender on behalf of the Emperor and the Japanese government. Four minutes later, General MacArthur signed to accept the surrender on behalf of the Allied Powers. The instrument of surrender signed on this day was based upon the protocols laid out in the Potsdam Declaration of 26 July 1945. These protocols called for the military occupation of Japan, war crimes trials, democratisation, the breaking up of cartels, the establishment of human rights, and the permanent demilitarisation of the country. For Japan, the surrender marked a moment of deep national shame, but also a new beginning.

On the day of the formal surrender, Japanese forces still totalled some 6,983,000 troops, of which 3,532,000 were stationed in the home islands. Despite Japanese forces being spread far and wide, 'in a great arc from Manchuria to the Solomons, and across the islands of the Central and Southwest Pacific', demobilisation was carried out remarkably quickly and with a minimum of friction. In Japan itself, the process had started before the American occupying authorities arrived, and within the space of three months demobilisation was all but complete. The smoothness of the process was characterised by an incident involving a young lieutenant from the American 43rd Infantry Division who was riding in a jeep along the road from Kazo to Kumagaya during the initial occupation period. Having spotted a cloud of dust in the distance, the young officer decided to investigate. It transpired that the dust had been kicked up by a Japanese tank column on its way to a demobilisation point. As the jeep approached the column, the lead tank stopped to let it pass. Skirting around the tank, the jeep's driver soon found that he was in trouble as the soft shoulder of the road crumbled away leaving the vehicle mired in the clinging mud of a rice paddy. A Japanese officer came running up to investigate, and speaking in broken English asked if the tank crew had been at fault. Following assurances to the contrary, the Japanese officer ordered the tank crew to pull the jeep out of the mud using their towing cable. Only weeks before, such an incident would have been unthinkable. It was also highly significant that the Japanese tank column was allowed to proceed to the demobilisation point independently, a sign that the 'Americans and the Japanese alike were integrated in a demobilisation programme which was evidently successful.'

The remarkably successful demobilisation programme would have had little real meaning had it not gone hand in hand with a process of demilitarisation which aimed at removing Japan's capacity to wage war. Considerable quantities of war *materiel* had been dispersed along the coast, in ports, defensive installations, warehouses, tunnels and caves. Notwithstanding the difficulties raised by the dispersal of supplies, munitions, and weaponry, demilitarisation had been effectively completed by the time the new Japanese constitution was announced in November 1946. This remarkable achievement would not have been possible without the full cooperation of the Japanese authorities.

One of the most successful aspects of demilitarisation was the near complete destruction of the Japanese tank and mechanised forces. Only a few tanks and armoured vehicles survived the cull. During August 1945, two Chi-To tanks were dumped in Lake Hamana by the Japanese authorities who did not want them to fall into the enemy's hands. The occupying authorities managed to recover one of the tanks as they were interested in discovering how far Japanese tank technology had progressed. What they saw impressed them greatly, as the Chi-To combined firepower, mobility and armour protection in a design clearly inspired by the German Panther tank. To this day the second Chi-To remains in the lake despite efforts by local volunteers and a marine survey company to locate the tank in a series of recovery attempts made between November 2012 and February 2013.

Along with the Chi-To recovered by the occupation authorities, a partially completed Chi-Ri tank was also retained for inspection. Both models were subsequently shipped to the Aberdeen Proving Grounds where they were eventually scrapped in 1952. In Japan, only one Chi-Nu tank survived the scrapping process. Today it is on display at the Ground Self-Defence Force Military Ordnance Training School at Tsuchiura, Japan. Arguably, the finest collection of surviving Japanese tanks and armoured fighting vehicles can be found at the Kubinka Tank Museum (Museum Hall N7) in the Russian Federation. For British readers, it may be of interest to note that Bovington Tank Museum has a Ha-Go tank on display. This particular tank is one of approximately twenty-five surviving examples and one of only two which are still in running order. During the 2019 Tank Festival at Bovington, visitors were given a rare opportunity to see this Ha-Go running around the test track.

It is only when standing next to a Ha-Go that the realisation dawns that these were hardly tanks at all. Compared to a Sherman or a T-34 they are positively Lilliputian. One wonders at the bravery displayed by Japanese tank crews when they were faced with the behemoths fielded by their more technologically advanced enemies. In China, there was far less opposition to Japan's tank forces, and as such it should be remembered that the light two or three-man tanks developed during the 1930s proved to be very effective in the infantry support role. Later, the larger Chi-Ha medium tank which represented an improvement on the rather antiquated tanks developed in the late 1920s and early 1930s went on to prove its worth during operations in China, although it must be said that his theatre of operations was hardly a suitable proving ground. The shortcomings of the Chi-Ha, namely the installation of the same low velocity 57 mm tank gun as used on the I-Go, riveted construction, and relatively thin armour were vulnerabilities that would sooner or later be exposed by Allied tanks.

The crushing defeat at Nomonhan at the hands of the Soviets should have been a wake-up call for the Japanese tank forces. Moreover, the spectacular success of the German panzer formations in 1940 showed how far Japan had fallen behind in terms of combined-arms doctrine and technology. By the time decisions were made to modernise the Japanese tank forces, priorities for raw materials had shifted almost entirely in favour of the Navy and Air Force. In 1942, some improvements were made to the Chi-Ha tank such as the installation of a 47 mm high-velocity tank gun. This weapon gave the tank a fighting chance against the heavier Allied models, particularly when it was deployed in an ambush position. Having said that, in terms of tank-versus-tank combat on the open battlefield, Japanese tanks remained very much at a disadvantage right through until the bitter end of the conflict in August 1945.

Appendices

Appendix 1
The Kungchuling Mixed Brigade

For all the successes of tanks employed during the Jehol campaign in 1933, the Army Staff in Tokyo continued to regard them purely as an adjunct to the infantry. In Manchuria, the wide-open spaces prompted some officers into envisioning a more independent role for tanks based around a formation which would include motorised infantry, artillery, engineer and support elements. To this end, the 1st Independent Mixed Brigade was formed in Kungchuling in 1934. This new unit was based around the recently formed 4th Tank Battalion that consisted of three tank companies, each holding fifteen light tanks, a headquarters with three more light tanks, and a depot which held ten more light tanks in reserve. The motorised infantry element consisted of a tankette company, three infantry battalions, a battalion gun company, three artillery batteries, an engineer company, and a flamethrower platoon equipped with five specialised assault tanks. The 3rd Tank Battalion (also stationed at Kungchuling) was not an organic part of the unit, but some elements of it frequently took part in trials during the development phase.

The Kungchuling Brigade was at best only a partial success. On the vast unpaved Manchurian steppes, the wheeled vehicles could not keep up with the tanks. The engineer unit attached to the brigade had been formed primarily to undertake an assault role and as a consequence was of little help in assisting the brigade to traverse the difficult terrain. There were also frequent mechanical breakdowns caused by the fragility of machinery that was not robust enough to withstand the rigours of a Manchurian winter.

In 1937, the brigade participated in operations in northern China. Here too the terrain was often difficult and as a consequence the tanks were frequently unable to keep pace with the infantry. Not surprisingly, infantry officers complained about a lack of tank cooperation. These complaints caught the attention of conservative senior Army commanders whose inbuilt prejudices led to the continued shackling of these unsuitable tanks to the infantry in a support role. Lieutenant-General Kōji Sakai who commanded a tank brigade was so aggrieved by the situation that took his complaints direct to the Quhar Expeditionary Army Commander General Hideki Tojo. In the event he could no have picked a worse person to go to as Tojo was a staunch traditionalist. It was therefore no surprise that Sakai's decision to approach Tojo backfired, his complaints only serving to sour relations to such an extent that he was dismissed and the brigade disbanded shortly thereafter.

Appendix 2
The Yasuoka Detachment

Japanese intelligence failures regarding the strength of Soviet tank forces on the Soviet-Manchurian border led the Kwantung Army viewing any coming confrontation as being largely a battle fought by opposing infantry units. Back in Tokyo, the Japanese leadership appeared to be slightly more cognisant of the threat and accordingly issued orders through the Army High Command for the strengthening of Manchuria's borders with Mongolia and the Soviet Union. To this end, the 3rd and 4th Tank Regiments arrived in the Nomonhan area with a combined strength of three medium tank companies, three light tank companies, and accompanying headquarters and supply companies. Subsequently, the two Regiments were amalgamated into the 'Yasuoka Detachment.'

Named after its commander Lieutenant-General Masaomi Yasuoka, the detachment consisted of the two tank regiments, motorised infantry, and artillery and engineer components. In theory, the broad Manchurian plains offered the ideal opportunity to put into practice combined-arms theory. But in reality, the limited combined-arms capability of the Japanese forces meant that synchronisation of the various elements proved almost impossible. During the assault towards the east bank of the Khalkin Gol in July 1939, Japanese tanks outran their supporting elements and so ended up 'fighting naked and alone.' The fighting at Nomonhan, clearly demonstrated that the infantry and artillery were 'totally incapable of keeping up with the tanks.' Notwithstanding, the Kwantung Army leadership placed the blame for operational failures squarely with the tank regiment's commanders. These criticisms may well have contributed to the decision to disband the unit in 1940.

Appendix 3
Tank Groups

The German *Blitzkrieg* in France and the Low Countries made even the most conservative Japanese generals recognise the potential of armoured forces. Their calls for the reorganisation and expansion of Japanese tank forces were soon answered with the formation in Manchuria of the 1st Tank Group at Tungning and the 2nd Tank Group at Tungan. Each group consisted of three tank regiments. Their primary mission of providing infantry support hardly served to emulate German tactics, but at least it was a start.

For the time being at least, tanks were to remain firmly wedded to the infantry. Regimental tank commanders were given little latitude, and in circumstances when tanks were allocated directly to an infantry unit, their duties were clearly defined:

> When the tanks are allotted directly to infantry units, the tank regimental commander gives the general outline of the plan of action, leaving the details of execution to the tank company commanders. For example, if it is necessary for the tanks to execute a reversal of movement to facilitate the forward advance of the infantry, the movement is made on order of the tank company commanders, often in response to a direct request from the infantry for the manoeuvre.

In different circumstances such as when tanks were given specific objectives, the tank regimental commander kept control throughout the operation. This method of tank–infantry cooperation was favoured when time limitations made it difficult to react to changes in the battlefield situation.

The catalyst for the reorganisation process was the German panzer divisions that had achieved their remarkable successes by attacking *en masse*. There is some irony to be found in the force structure and deployment plans developed by the Japanese in that they closely resembled those which had been adopted by the defeated French army rather than those of the victorious German forces whom they wished to emulate.

Appendix 4
The 1941 Army Mobilisation Plan

The Army Mobilisation Plan for 1941 set out to standardise tables of organisation and equipment for the tank group headquarters, regular medium and light tank regiments, ammunition trains and maintenance companies. The ammunition supply for the medium tank component reflected the infantry support role assigned to armoured units. For each armour piercing round issued, two high explosive rounds were furnished. The equipment levels in the new plan continued to exist largely on paper as additional tank units were continuously being formed. By 1940, fifteen tank regiments had been raised, and over the following year, the 1st, 6th, 9th, 11th, and 23rd Tank Regiments were added. This accumulation in overall strength looked good on paper, but in reality was illusionary as some of the regiments (including those recently formed) fielded obsolete I-Go medium tanks. Command and control of the tank regiments in Manchuria would also have been very difficult in operational situations due to an acute shortage of radio sets.

In November 1941, a major redistribution of tank forces took place with the formation of the 3rd Tank Group which was subordinated to the 25th Army for the invasion of Malaya. At the same time, the 4th Tank Regiment was transferred from Manchuria, and the 7th Tank Regiment from China for operations in the Philippines. During Japan's southerly drive, the tank regiments performed well, particularly in Malaya. Following the fall of Singapore and the withdrawal of American forces into their Bataan fortress, Japanese tank formations were freed up for reallocation. By mid-1942, only two light tank regiments remained in the newly occupied territories.

Appendix 5
Tank Divisions

The Formation of Japanese Tank Divisions

In an attempt to emulate the success of the German panzers, the Imperial General Headquarters ordered the formation of the Mechanised Army. In July 1942, the 1st and 2nd Tank Groups, the 1st, 2nd, 4th, 7th and 12th Independent Anti-Tank Companies, the main body of the 1st Independent Field Artillery Regiment, the 27th, 28th and 29th Independent Anti-Aircraft Companies, the 16th and 18th Field Machine Cannon Companies, the main body of the 5th Independent Engineer Regiment and the 3rd Heavy River Crossing Company were all assigned to this new formation. Perhaps the thinking around this grouping was a little too far advanced as technical and operational realities meant that the history of the Mechanised Army was over before it had even begun. Quite correctly, the Kwantung Army regarded the new Mechanised Army as being too unwieldy. Therefore, the formation was disbanded and its constituent parts reorganised into a force structure based around more effective divisional sized, self-contained units.

The 1st Tank Division was formed in Ningan, Manchuria, in June 1942. It consisted of the 1st Tank Brigade (1st and 5th Tank Regiments) and the 2nd Tank Brigade (3rd and 9th Tank Regiments). The 2nd Tank Division was formed at Kungchuling, Manchuria, in June 1942. It consisted of the 3rd Tank Brigade (6th and 7th Tank Regiments) and the 4th Tank Brigade (10th and 11th Tank Regiments). During this period, overall personnel numbers for the new divisions almost doubled. There were also notable increases in equipment and supplies. Moreover, increased levels of anti-tank protection and allocation of the Shinhoto Chi-Ha all served to give these new divisions a sharper cutting edge.

The formation of the first two tank divisions came at a time when overall tank production was reaching a wartime peak. Thereafter, it entered a precipitous decline as priorities shifted towards the construction of more aircraft and ships. As a consequence, the formation of divisional-sized units was restricted. In December 1942, the 3rd Tank Division was formed in Baotou, China. The division consisted of the 5th Tank Brigade (8th and 12th Tank Regiments) and the 6th Tank Brigade (13th and 17th Tank Regiments). The addition of a third tank division was an organisational improvement, but it did little to increase overall numbers of fighting machines as older models held by the regiments were gradually being replaced by newer and more effective tanks. Shortages of new tanks meant that no new tank divisions were formed in 1943. Thereafter the situation continued to deteriorate to the extent that Japan could only find the resources to form one more divisional-sized unit before the end of the war.

The 4th Tank Division was raised in July 1944 in Chiba Province, Japan. This formation never reached the status of the earlier divisions. It lacked the infantry and artillery components which would have made it a self-contained combined-arms unit, although to some extent these deficiencies were compensated by an abundance of experience, skills, equipment and supplies. The division was created from the students and staff of the Chiba Tank School, making it the rough equivalent of the German Panzer Lehr Division. The 28th, 29th and 30th Tank Regiments around which the division was formed had an entirely new structure which included large pioneer elements in lieu of regular infantry.

On paper, the division appeared to be a powerful force as it was equipped with the new Chi-Nu medium tank and Ho-Ni III tank destroyers. These modern machines may have given the division a sharp cutting edge, but it still suffered from the same deficiencies in motorised transport which had affected the operations of all other Japanese tank formations. Furthermore, the three tank regiments had only been supplied with 'nominal' maintenance companies whose logistical and support arrangements where wholly inadequate for the task in hand. It is therefore questionable as to whether this division would have made a significant contribution the defence of the homeland.

Organisation

The Japanese tank divisions may have been inspired by the German panzer formations which had wreaked havoc in Poland, France and the Soviet Union, but they never got the opportunity to fight in the same way. Time and time again, tank regiments and other units were siphoned off, leaving the divisions unbalanced and lacking in combined-arms capability. In February 1944, an attempt was made to standardise the force structure of the tank divisions by creating 'triangular units' with three regimental headquarters and three brigade headquarters instead of the previous four. At the same time the remaining regiments were reinforced with new tanks. However, no two divisions were organised or equipped in exactly the same way as much depended on 'the commander's preferences and the equipment available.

Combat History

In March 1944, the 1st Tank Division's 9th Tank Regiment was sent to Saipan where it was subsequently destroyed. The following month, the division's 3rd Tank Regiment was transferred to China, leaving it with only two tank regiments. In March 1945, the division was transferred to the homeland island of Kyushu. Here it was augmented by the 1st Tank Regiment of the 3rd Tank Division. The reinforced division was then tasked with holding a line from Mount Tsukuba to the Tama River. The surrender of Japan on 15 August 1945 meant that the country was occupied rather than fought over. Within a short space of time, the three intact regiments of the division were demobilised without incident.

In February 1944, the 2nd Tank Division's 11th Tank Regiment was transferred to the Kuriles. The following month, the reconnaissance unit (renamed as the 27th Tank Regiment) and the anti-aircraft unit were deployed to China. In July 1944, the division was reduced in strength prior to its deployment to Luzon. The reason behind this reduction appears to have been to conserve valuable shipping space. On arrival in Luzon, the division was broken up and assigned to different commands. In January 1945, its remnants were destroyed without having changed the course of the battle.

The 3rd Tank Division remained in China as a mobile reserve for the entire course of the war. From April 1944 it participated in the massive Ichi-Go operation in central and southern China. In light of the limited anti-tank capabilities of the Chinese forces, the division was equipped to a lower standard than the others. Notwithstanding the division's deficiencies in artillery and anti-tank support, it made a significant contribution to operations in this vast theatre. Masao Yamamoto, a young officer in the division later recalled some of his experiences:

> My military career began in December 1938 when I entered the preparatory course at the Imperial Military Academy at Ichigaya in Tokyo ... During

the latter part of the first year, I chose to specialise as a cavalryman ... In April 1940, I entered the Officer Training School at Zama ... In response to the changing times, the cavalry course shifted emphasis from horsemanship towards mechanisation. When I took it, only three months of the fifteen were devoted to horsemanship, and after that the emphasis was on tank warfare.

When I graduated in July 1941, I was sent to North China and took up my duties with a tank unit. It was a unit that specialised in bandit suppression, and served in ordinary combat, with troops sent to hold a position in battle. It achieved positive results ... Just before Pearl Harbor, I was transferred from that unit to the tank school just outside Chiba City for what in the United States would be called a basic officers' course. In March 1942, I was scheduled to return to my unit, but I was suddenly ordered to take part in bandit suppression operations. That turned out to be my baptism under enemy fire ... Fortunately the tank I was driving passed the test of battle ... If I had not succeeded in this test, I would certainly have had to overcome various problems later on.

Captain Yamamoto was fortunate to survive the war. In August 1945, the Japanese empire in China collapsed overnight. He was one of the many thousands taken prisoner following Japan's capitulation to the Allied powers. Some of his unit's tanks continued in service for many years with the Chinese People's Liberation Army following the defeat of Chiang's nationalist forces in 1949.

In August 1945, the 4th Tank Division began the process of demobilisation following the American occupation of Japan. This division was the first to possess tanks that could knock out enemy tanks without having to resort to close range ambush tactics, but it lacked the logistical back up to make it a truly mobile formation. Perhaps as Leland Ness opines, the Japanese High Command 'failed to comprehend the magnitude of logistical problems attendant on an armoured force, or they simply gave up and restricted their tanks to the infantry support role and the defence of the homeland.' The answer has to be a bit of both. Japan's limited industrial base could not properly support the nation's armoured forces, therefore tank units offensive capabilities were limited due to weakly armed and armoured machines and insufficient logistical back up. With this in mind, retaining the 4th Tank Division for home defence was probably the most sensible option.

Appendix 6
Japanese Armoured Tactical Principles

Japanese armoured doctrine stressed aggressiveness and the need to make rapid decisions. Tank commanders were therefore expected to liaise with the infantry in order to facilitate the prompt exploitation of gains made either by armour or foot soldiers. Doctrine called for tanks that had outrun the infantry to return to the lines in order to coordinate their actions, though in practice this rarely happened as tank commanders' martial impulses often got the better of them. Because of this, Japanese tanks were time and time again left exposed to anti-tank fire directed by well-armed enemy infantry units.

Tank regiment attacks against defences in depth were usually carried out in three echelons. The first, under the direct control of the regimental commander cleared a path for the supporting infantry by neutralising enemy anti-tank guns and strongpoints. The second echelon, under the direct control of the infantry battalion commander focused on the neutralisation of enemy heavy-machine-gun positions. The third echelon was held in reserve positions where it waited for a favourable opportunity to exploit the breakthrough of the first two echelons.

Tanks were sometimes used to fix the enemy in position while combined-arms units skirted around the flanks. In the United States Army's updated Special Series No. 36 handbook on *Japanese Tank and Antitank Warfare* dated 1 August 1945, the use of tanks in close support roles and against hostile flanks is covered in detail:

> When the tank support for the infantry must be exceptionally close, some important modifications in Japanese tactics are made, including organisation of the tank regiment into two combat units. The first combat unit is divided into a left and right formation, each of which is preceded by a patrol of light tanks to develop the enemy position and draw antitank fire. Both the formations consist of four platoons arranged into two columns of two platoons each. The two front platoons advance with the infantry; the two rear platoons are used to swing around the flanks of the leading platoons to engage located enemy antitank weapons. Each of the two formations is followed by a platoon of engineers.
>
> The second combat unit consists of four platoons. One platoon is assigned the mission of neutralising antitank guns and self-propelled artillery. The remaining three platoons are assigned the mission of liquidating automatic weapons. One of them may be used as a reserve to exploit success. The regimental headquarters moves with this combat unit following the first platoon ...
>
> In the event that there are no primary tank objectives requiring immediate action, or their location cannot be ascertained, the tanks may be employed against the enemy's flanks ... Japanese tactical doctrine for a flank attack directs the infantry battalion commander to concentrate his firepower against the enemy antitank weapons. If necessary, details are sent forward to clear lanes for the passage of tanks through areas containing antitank

weapons or where antitank weapons can be expected. Japanese doctrine also emphasises the necessity for infantry to cover and protect the tanks from antitank fire. Despite the promulgation of this doctrine, unaccompanied Japanese tanks were sent against U.S. antitank weapons on Guadalcanal and were completely annihilated.

For all the hard lessons of Guadalcanal, tank-infantry cooperation remained a problem until the very end of the war. American intelligence assessments continually rated the Japanese armoured forces as being in a technologically backwards state and tactically inept. On Saipan, General Saito's suicidal night tank attack appeared to confirm American views on the competency of Japanese tank forces.

Conversely, American intelligence sources consistently rated the Japanese infantry very highly. The battle-hardened defenders of far flung atolls and islands were regarded as resourceful, skilful and tactically adept. Indeed, as the war wore on, the staying power of the Japanese defence rested more and more on the infantry. This was not necessarily a reflection of flawed doctrine, but a recognition of technological shortcomings, narrow administrative margins for supply, and difficult terrain. Over time, tank units lost what little independence they had enjoyed, and as the Americans closed in on Iwo Jima and Okinawa, Japanese tanks were reduced to being nothing more than adjuncts to the defending infantry's anti-tank arm.

In the 215 page handbook on *Japanese Tank and Antitank Warfare* (U.S. Military Intelligence Division, 1 August 1945) a mere fifteen lines were devoted to the subject of tanks in defence. Indeed, this very short section concludes with the words, 'In recent operations, the Japanese dug in their tanks and used them defensively as artillery and antitank weapons.' Certainly, while American intelligence sources had made note of changes in Japanese defensive doctrine, very little was done to counteract the more sophisticated methods being employed by Japanese commanders.

On Pacific atolls and islands, Japanese tanks formed part of the defence forces. Their task was to act as either mobile or static pillboxes which would be used to inflict the maximum amount of damage on the enemy. Some tanks were completely dug in 'with only the turret exposed to allow all-around fire.' The positions would be well camouflaged in areas where enemy tanks would be expected to advance. At close range, the 47 mm gun mounted on the Shinhoto Chi-ha was capable of disabling Allied tanks when aimed at the weaker side armour, or specific aiming points such as tracks, bogie wheels, hatches and observation/pistol ports. These dug in tanks were part of a mutually supporting system of defence designed to inflict the maximum amount of damage on the enemy. Some officers, most notably the charismatic Colonel Nishi would have preferred tanks to have been used in a 'roving fire brigade' role. Realistically, this was never a viable option as they simply would have been frittered away without achieving any tangible results. Using tanks in a static role made more sense as it fitted in with the overall strategy for island defence.

To a large extent, topography dictated how Japanese tanks were deployed on Pacific atolls and islands. On Tarawa, some Ha-Go tanks roamed the beaches while others were dug in. Many atolls were as Gordon L. Rottman and Akira Takizawa state, 'hardly more than low sandbars, with little room for manoeuvre and offering virtually no concealment for tanks from ground or air observation.' Therefore, only limited numbers of tanks were deployed to these far flung places. When counter-attacks were launched against American invasion forces, they were invariably delayed, giving the Marines ample time to get their anti-tank weapons ashore. As the August 1945 edition of the handbook on *Japanese Tanks and Antitank Warfare* states:

> The use of piecemeal, uncoordinated attacks may be due to physical impossibilities, lack of the proper means, a failure to understand the methods, or lack of training. In any event, one thing is paramount; to date the Japanese have not employed armour according to modern concepts.

Had the invasion of the Japanese home islands taken place, the significant quantities of modern armour available to the Mobile Shock Force may well have been employed *en masse* in a style emulating the classic panzer thrusts of 1940. Such was the intention, although it is highly questionable whether such tactics would have been feasible given the chronic lack of transport and weak logistical support available in the homeland in 1945.

For the carefully husbanded Japanese tank forces, the reality of fighting on home soil would have been a chastening lesson in the art of modern warfare. The 4th Tank Division may well have met the same fate as the German Panzer Lehr Division on which it was modelled. Massed American airpower, artillery and armour would have rendered the most advanced Japanese armoured forces put into the field all but impotent.

Appendix 7
Principal Japanese Tank Models

Experimental Tanks
Type 87 Experimental Tank No. 1 Chi- I
In 1925, it was agreed that the Japanese Army would be provided with a Tank Corps. To make this possible, the decision was made to end the reliance on imported tanks by designing and building domestic models. The Army's

particular requirements led the completion of Experimental Tank No. 1 in February 1927. The short time that it took to design and produce this twin turreted tank was a remarkable achievement considering that it was a first for Japanese industry. This achievement was all the more impressive given the lack of home grown designs in the Japanese motor industry. The design may have been influenced by current European trends, but it was clearly a domestic product. Although the tank was heavier and slower than planned, it performed well in tests, proving that Japan was now capable of producing models which matched those of more advanced nations. The Imperial Japanese Army General Staff Office was pleased with the overall test results, but harboured some concerns that the tank was too heavy to cross bridges and rivers in China. Consequently, they issued a new requirement for a lighter tank with a single turret. This decision would later be proved correct as the multi-turret concept turned out to be a dead end in terms of tank development. The Type 87 was not only a first for Japan, but it also undoubtedly served to enhance the nation's growing status as a leading innovator in terms of the development of armour.

Dimensions: 6.3 × 2.4 × 2.78m (20.6 × 7.87 × 9.12ft)
Weight: 20 tons
Crew: 5 (commander, gunner, loader, machine-gunner × 2)
Engine: Mitsubishi V8 petrol engine, 140 hp
Armour: 6–15 mm (0.23– 0.59 in)
Armament—57 mm tank gun, 2 × 7.2 mm machine guns

Type 89 Experimental Tank No. 2 Chi-Ro
The requirements of the General Staff Office were finally met with the production of the prototype Type 89 Experimental Tank No. 2 Chi-Ro in 1929. This design was so successful in tests that the Army immediately decided that it should be standardised and mass produced as their medium tank.

Dimensions: See Type 89 I-Go medium tank
Weight: 10 tons
Crew: 3 (commander, gunner, loader)
Engine: Daimler 6 cylinder petrol engine, 100 hp
Speed: 25 kph (15.5 mph)
Armour: 17 mm (0.66 in)
Armament: Type 90 57 mm low-velocity tank gun, 2 × Type 91 machine-guns

Light Tanks and Tankettes

Type 92 Cavalry Tank

The Type 92 Jyu-Sokosha cavalry tank entered production at the Ishikawajima Motor Works in 1933. Designed primarily for reconnaissance and close support, this tankette was designated as a heavy armoured car as it was operated by the cavalry rather than the infantry. The Type 92 may have been both very fast (40 kph) and highly manoeuvrable, but it was wholly unsuited to combat as its only armament consisted of one Type 92 heavy machine gun mounted in the turret, and one Type 97 light machine gun mounted in the hull. Moreover, the thin 6 mm armour on the riveted and poorly welded hull could be penetrated by both 30 and 50 calibre rounds. Nonetheless, the Type 92 saw extensive combat with the Kwantung Army, most notably at Harbin and Rehe. Between 1932 and 1937, 167 examples were built.

Dimensions: 3.95 × 1.63 × 1.92 m (12.95 × 5.35 × 6.34 ft)
Weight: 3.5 tons
Armament: 13.2 mm (0.52 in) Type 92 heavy machine-gun, 6.6 mm (0.25 in) Type 91 machine-gun
Armour: 6–12 mm (0.24–0.47 in)
Crew: 3 (commander/gunner, driver, hull-machine-gunner)
Engine: Mitsubishi/Ishikawajima 6 cylinder inline engine, 45 hp.
Speed: 40 kph (25 mph)
Range: 200 km (120 miles)

Type 94 Tankette

The Type 94 was born out of the desire of infantry commanders to have a vehicle similar to that operated by the cavalry for cargo transportation, reconnaissance and communications duties. The design by the Tokyo Gas Industry Company (from 1942 known as Hino Motors), embodied the general design features of the Type 92, but with modified Carden-Lloyd type suspension. During the late 1920s and early 1930s a fad for tankettes developed in Europe. As such, it can be said that the Type 94 was clearly influenced by the British Carden-Lloyd design which was license-built by several countries. The Soviet T-27 and the Italian L3/33 and L3/35 models may also have influenced Japanese designers. The Type 94 was larger than the Carden-Lloyd and came equipped with a tracked trailer for transporting supplies. This capability meant that it was designated as a Tokushu Keninsha (Special Tractor). Later models were built without the tracked trailer as the vehicle proved to be an inexpensive means of providing troops in China with fire support. Between 1935 and 1937, 823 examples were built, including a specialised chemical warfare version which could dispense mustard gas.

Dimensions: 3.08 × 1.62 × 1.62 m (10.10 × 5.3 × 5.3 ft)
Weight: 3.5–3.58 tons
Crew: 2 (commander/gunner, driver)
Engine: Mitsubishi air-cooled 4-cylinder petrol engine, 32 hp
Speed: 40 kph (25 mph)
Armour: 4–12 mm (0.15–0.47 in)
Armament: 6.5 mm (0.25 in) Type 91 machine-gun, or 7.7 mm (0.303 in)
  Type 92 machine-gun
Range: 200 km (162miles)

Type 97 Tankette

The Type 97 Te-Ke tankette was designed as a fast reconnaissance vehicle to replace the earlier Type 94. Although bearing some similarities to its predecessor, the Type 97 had a redesigned hull and turret which showed 'a definite attempt on the part of the Japanese to design a simpler front plate and to improve the deflection angles of their armour.' The enlarged turret constructed from rolled armour plate provided sufficient space to mount a 37 mm tank gun. This step up in armament marked a vast improvement on the machine guns mounted on previous models, although the turret-mounted machine gun was retained on some models as it was more effective against infantry than a cannon.

Typically, six Type 97s were distributed to each infantry division. Most saw action in China where they came up against Mao's Italian built tankettes and aged French tanks of First World War vintage. At Nomonhan, a handful of Type 97s faced Soviet BT-5 and BT-7 light tanks. Totally outclassed, the Type 97s were destroyed by the heavier and more technologically advanced Soviet tanks. This rapidly obsolescent model fared better in Malaya and the Philippines where its light weight and high levels of manoeuvrability enabled it to make significant contributions to both campaigns. Between 1939 and 1942 some 596 (approximate) examples were built including the Type 98 So-Da armoured personnel and ammunition carrier, the Type 100 Te-Re artillery observation vehicle, the Type 97 disinfecting vehicle and the Type 97 gas scattering vehicle.

Dimensions: 3.07 × 1.80 × 1.77 m (12 × 5.10 × 5.9 ft)
Weight: 4.7 tons
Crew: 2 (commander/gunner, driver)
Engine: Hino Motors diesel air-cooled 4-cylinder engine, 48 hp
Armour: 4–16 mm (0.16–0.63 in)
Armament: 37 mm (1.46 in) Type 94 tank gun, or 7.7 mm (0.3 in) Type 97
  machine-gun
Range—200 km (155 miles)

Type 95 Light Tank

The Type 95 Ha-Go light tank was designed to meet an Army specification for a light tank capable of keeping pace with the motorised infantry. In June 1934 a prototype model was completed at the Army's Sagami Arsenal. Following field tests with the Kwantung Army in Manchuria some modifications were made which resulted in the completion of a second prototype in November 1935. The tank performed well enough in China, but proved vulnerable to close-in attack by infantry armed with grenades and Molotov cocktails. At Nomonhan, the larger and more heavily armed Soviet tanks took a heavy toll on the weaker and more lightly armed Type 95s. Despite this tank's evident shortcomings, it remained in production until 1943.

Between 1939 and 1943 some 2,300 examples were built by Sagami Arsenal, Hitachi Industries, Niigata Tekkosho, Kobe Seikosho, Kukura Arsenal and Mitsubishi Heavy Industries. With the Ha-Go having been produced in greater numbers than any other Japanese tank it became a ubiquitous presence on the battlefield. It performed particularly well in Malaya where it appeared in unexpected places in a supposedly inaccessible jungle environment.

Variants and derivatives of the Ha-Go included the Type 4 Ke-Nu which was fitted with an early Chi-Ha turret mounting a low-velocity 57 mm tank gun (approximately 100 examples were constructed in 1944). These tanks saw limited combat in Manchuria and Korea in August 1945. Today, a surviving example is on display at the Kubinka Tank Museum in Moscow. The Ke-Ri was an experimental model slated to replace the Ha-Go in 1942. It retained the entire chassis of its predecessor, but had a new turret mounting a high-velocity 47 mm tank gun. The Type 2 Ka-Mi was an adaptation of the Ha-Go which was specially tailored to meet the needs of the Special Naval Landing Forces. Over the course of a production run spanning two years (1942–43) 184 examples were built.

Dimensions: 4.38 × 2.06 × 2.18 m (14.4 × 6.8 × 7.2 ft)
Weight: 7.4 tons
Crew: 3 (commander/gunner, driver, machine-gunner)
Engine: Mitsubishi A6120VD, air-cooled diesel, 120 hp
Armament: 37 mm (1.46 in) Type 94 tank gun, 2 × Type 97 7.7 mm (0.3 in) machine-guns
Armour: 6–16 mm (0.24–0.63 in)
Speed: 45kph (28 mph)
Range: 250 km (155 miles)

Type 89 Medium Tank

The Type 89 I-Go medium tank evolved from Japan's first attempt to design and produce an indigenous model after several years of experimenting with foreign designs. The early Type 89A version was powered by a petrol engine, while the Type 89B version featured a more revolutionary diesel engine. The design was very much of its time, featuring a tall slab-sided hull and an irregularly shaped turret. The multiple bogie suspension was derived from the British Vickers C design. Following the I-Go's initial production run in 1931, continual improvements were made, most notably the installation of a 57 mm tank gun in 1937. However, by 1939 the model was fast approaching obsolescence. During the border conflicts with the Soviet Union, the weak armour of the I-Go would be cruelly exposed by the Red Army's T-26 and BT series tanks.

By 1941 it was clear that the I-Go was obsolete. The following year they were gradually withdrawn from service. In the meantime, significant numbers saw action in the Philippines, Malaya and Burma. When carrying out exploitation and pursuit operations these tanks proved to be very effective, although it was clear that their days were numbered following the first encounters with Allied tanks such as the M3 Stuart. In total, some 409 I-Go tanks were produced. The I-Go may have been a somewhat antiquated design which was firmly rooted in the 1920s, nonetheless it represented a significant milestone in Japanese tank development.

Dimensions: 5.73 × 2.13 × 2.5 m (18.79 × 7.8 × 8.4 ft)
Weight: 9.9 tons
Crew: 4 (commander, driver, loader, gunner)
Armament: Type 90 57 mm (2.24 in) tank gun, 2 × Type 91 6.5 mm machine-guns
Armour: 6–17 mm (0.24–0.67 in)
Engine: Daimler 6-cylinder, air-cooled petrol engine, 118 hp
Speed: 16 kph (10 mph)
Range: 150 km (95 miles)

Type 97 Chi-Ha/Shinhoto Chi-Ha Medium Tank

The Type 97 Chi-Ha medium tank ran a close second to the Ha-Go in terms of production numbers with 2,100 examples being built between 1938 and 1943. When it first appeared in China and Manchuria in 1938, the Chi-Ha was a tank which held much promise. The following year, the Chi-Ha clashed with Soviet armour at Nomonhan where the tank's low-velocity main armament proved to be all but useless. After Nomonhan, it was still thought that the basic design remained sound, and therefore the same part riveted part welded design that had been abandoned by both the Germans and the Allies was retained. The only real improvement made on an otherwise obsolescent design was the addition of a 47 mm high-velocity gun in an enlarged turret. Some 930 examples of these Shinhoto (improved) Chi-Ha tanks were produced before production ended in late 1943. This tank was meant to be no more than a stop-gap measure until heavier models were produced. Instead, it became Japan's main medium tank until the end of the war. Heavier models were indeed produced, but all were reserved for homeland defence.

Dimensions: Chi-Ha 5.5 × 2.34 × 2.33 m (18 × 7.6 × 7.5 ft); Chi -Ha (improved) 5.5 × 2.38 × 2.33 m (18 × 7.8 × 7.5 ft)
Weight: Chi-Ha 15 tons; Chi-Ha (improved) 16.5 tons
Crew: 4 (commander, gunner, loader, machine-gunner)
Engine: Mitsubishi Type 97 diesel V12, 170 hp
Speed: 38 kph (23 mph)
Armour: 12–25 mm (0.14–0.47 in)
Armament: Chi-Ha Type 97 57 mm (2.24 in) low-velocity tank gun, 2 × Type 97 7.7 mm machine-guns; Chi-Ha (improved) Type 1 47 mm high-velocity tank gun, 2 × Type 97 7.7 mm machine-guns
Range: 210kph (165 miles)

Type 3 Chi-Nu Medium Tank
Following reports of encounters with Allied tanks it became clear that the improved version of the Chi-Ha mounting a 47 mm high-velocity tank gun was outclassed by the ubiquitous Sherman. Therefore, the Imperial General Headquarters decided to develop a new medium tank. Having recognised that an entirely new design would take time to develop and produce, a stop-gap design based on the existing Chi-Ha chassis was approved. Design work on the Type 3 Chi-Nu was completed in October 1943. The finished design still resembled the Chi-Ha, but had a larger turret to accommodate a more effective Type 4 75 mm tank gun. The Chi-Nu was the final development of the outdated Chi-Ha chassis, but wartime shortages and shifting production priorities meant that production was delayed until 1944. As a result of this production delay, the Chi-Nu was by the end of the war the heaviest and most sophisticated model in Japanese service.

Dimensions: 6.73 × 2.87 × 2.87 m (22 × 9.5 × 9.5 ft)
Weight: 19.1 tons
Crew: 5 (commander, driver, gunner, loader, hull machine-gunner/radio operator)
Engine: Mitsubishi Type 100, V-12 diesel, 240 hp
Speed: 39 kph (24 mph)
Armour: 12–50 mm (0.47–1.97 in)
Armament: 75 mm (2.95 in) Type 3 tank gun, 1 × Type 97 7.7 mm (0.3 in) machine-gunner
Range: 210 km (130 miles)

Appendix 8
Principal Self-Propelled Guns and Tank Destroyers

Type 1 Ho-Ni 1

The creation of Japanese armoured divisions in 1942 generated a requirement for mechanised artillery. As the design and development of an entirely new vehicle would have been both time and cost intensive, a more straightforward solution was required. The existing Type 97 tank chassis was an ideal platform on which to mount heavier guns capable of both providing infantry support and of destroying enemy tanks. The first conversion of a Type 97 chassis took place in June 1941, followed by a limited production run of twenty-six examples the following year. The Ho-Ni 1 was used operationally during the fighting on Luzon following the American landings in January 1945, but there were too few available to make much of an impression on the battlefield. Perhaps more priority should have been given to the production of the Ho-Ni 1 as the design which was influenced by the success of the German Marder series was essentially sound.

Dimensions: 5.9 × 2.29 × 2.39 m (19.36 × 7.51 × 7.84 ft)
Weight: 15.4 tons
Crew: 5 (commander, driver, gun crew × 3)
Engine: Mitsubishi Type 97 diesel V12, 170 hp
Speed: 38 kph (25 mph)
Armour: 25–51 mm (0.98–2 in)
Armament: 76 mm (3 in) Type 90 gun
Range: 200 km (160 miles)

Type 1 Ho-Ni II

The Ho-Ni I was supplanted by the Ho-Ni II in July 1942 following the production of the first prototype model, although serial production was delayed until the following year. The basic design was similar to the Ho-Ni 1, retaining the three-sided gun shield which left the crew's rear exposed. The Ho-Ni II served operationally in the Philippines and Burma.

Dimensions: 5.55 × 2.29 × 2.39 m (18.2 × 7.51 × 7.84 ft)
Weight: 16.1 tons
Crew: 5 (commander, driver, gun crew × 3)
Engine: Mitsubishi Type 97 diesel V12, 170 hp
Speed: 38 kph (25 mph)
Armour: 25–51 mm (0.98–2 in)
Armament: 105 mm (4.13 in) Type 91 howitzers
Range: 200 km (160 miles)

Type 1 Ho-Ni III

The Ho-Ni III represented an improvement on previous models as it mounted a powerful tank gun that was capable of knocking out Shermans and T-34s at medium-long range. Crew protection was also improved with the addition of a new overhanging gun shield which completely enclosed the fighting compartment. Production of these so-called 'gun tanks' was entrusted to Hitachi who turned out the new model at a painfully slow rate. Eventually, the contract to produce fifty-seven examples was fulfilled, but the difficulties experienced in doing so clearly demonstrated that Japanese industry was incapable of producing enough new tanks to keep the armoured force current. For a nation whose factories were seriously overstretched, gun tanks proved to be an expedient method to provide tank regiments with the additional firepower they needed without placing additional strain on the creaking industrial complex.

Dimensions: 5.52 × 2.29 × 2.39 m (18.7 × 7.6 × 7.10 ft)
Weight: 17 tons
Crew: 5 (commander, driver, gun crew × 3)
Engine: Mitsubishi Type 97 diesel V12, 170 hp
Armour: 12–25 mm (0.47–0.98 in)
Armament: 75 mm (2.95 in) Type 3 gun
Range: 200 km (160 miles)

Appendix 9
Japanese Tank and Armoured Fighting Vehicle Production 1931–1945

Japanese tank and armoured fighting vehicle production began in earnest following the Army's adoption of the Type 89 medium tank in 1929. Production was slow as the Sagami Arsenal subcontracted much of the work. As a consequence there was little standardisation in the Type 89 fleet. Inevitably, the Type 89 'suffered from the shortcomings of any first-of-a-kind product.' Over time, a number of small changes were introduced, but this rather antiquated design proved to be a dead-end in terms of further development. Apart from the introduction of the diesel engine in the Type 89B, the obsolete features of this indigenous medium tank contributed very little to later Japanese tank designs.

The Army next turned to lighter vehicles at a time when tankettes were all the vogue in Europe. These small, light, two-man vehicles were usually armed with a single machine-gun and were intended primarily for the supply and reconnaissance role. Japan became one of the most prolific manufacturers and users of the tankette. While these small vehicles could be quite useful, their light armour had led many European armies to abandon the concept by the outbreak of war in 1939. Italy was a notable exception, remaining steadfastly faithful to tankettes. In July and August 1941, a number of domestically produced L3 models were dispatched to the Russian Front. The tankette soldiered on too in the Japanese Army, although most were relegated to support roles.

In 1935, the Army formally accepted the Ha-Go light tank, but within five years it was already obsolete by world standards. Nevertheless, production of this small under-gunned tank continued into 1943. Approximately 2,300 examples were built by Mitsubishi Heavy Industries, Sugami Arsenal, Hitachi Industries, Niigata Tekkoshu, Kobe Seikosho and the Kokura Arsenal.

The lightly armed and armoured Japanese tanks and tankettes were clearly inadequate for the projected major combat operations against the Soviet Union. Despite this, some conservative elements within the Army attempted to stymie the development of a new medium tank to replace the rapidly ageing Type 89 medium tank. Their lack of enthusiasm however failed to prevent the development of a next-generation tank.

In 1938 the Chi-Ha medium tank entered serial production at the Kokura and Osaka facilities. By September 1939 300 units had been produced (a pitifully low number by European standards). The Chi-Ha performed well enough in China against the poorly-armed Nationalist forces, but later when faced with a first class military power fared badly. At Nomonhan in July–August 1939, the more heavily armed Soviet BT tanks exposed the Chi-Ha's inherent vulnerabilities. This chastening experience led to the development of a 47 mm tank gun and new turret which could drop onto the hull of the Type 97. The resulting marriage of the existing hull with the new turret configuration was known as the Shinhoto Chi-Ha medium tank. Deliveries of the new tank began in early 1942, by which time the design was already obsolete by world standards.

In February 1944, production shifted fully towards the Type 1 Chi-He which was a rather belated attempt to modernise the Chi-Ha by using more resilient welded armour and a more powerful engine. The switchover inevitably led to production difficulties. Between February and August 1944 an average of twenty Chi-He medium tanks were turned out every month. This paltry figure could do little to redress the technological imbalance which Japan's tank forces faced in the field. What was needed was a new tank which could take on enemy armour on more equal terms.

Work had already started on such a tank, and in September 1944 the Chi-Nu which represented the final development of the Chi-Ha went into production. The Chi-Nu was essentially a stop-gap design which would suffice until the substantially larger Chi-To was ready for serial production. The Chi-To was the most sophisticated Japanese tank to reach the production stage. Plans to manufacture this Japanese variant of the German Panther medium tank were drawn up with a projected twenty units being turned out by Mitsubishi Heavy Industries and five at the Kobe-Seiko facility per month. Japanese industry was simply incapable of producing this sophisticated tank in anything like the quantities required, and by August 1945 only six chassis and two finished tanks had been completed.

An even more powerful tank broadly based on the heavy German Tiger tank was on the drawing board. But in May 1945, the Chi-Ri concept was abandoned in favour of the Chi-To after one semi-completed prototype had been produced. Finally, Japanese tank designs had caught up with those of the other major warring powers. Had the Chi-Nu and Chi-Ri been produced in quantity they would have posed a potent threat to the tank supremacy of the Allied nations (assuming of course that sufficient logistical support was provided). The lessons of Nomonhan, the *Blitzkrieg*, Kursk, Burma, the Philippines, and Saipan took a long time to permeate the conservative Japanese Army, and by the time they had been translated into modern tank designs, it was a case of too little, too late. Consequently, the war would be fought with suicidal bravery by tank forces equipped with largely obsolete tanks. Facing them were the lavishly equipped American, British-Commonwealth, and Soviet tank forces.

Not since King Leonidas I of Sparta led his men against the might of the Empire of Xerxes at Thermopylae has there been a more unequal contest. Japanese industry had succeeded in producing the fifth largest tank force in the world in 1940. Numbers however mean little when those tanks were underpowered, weakly armed and thinly armoured machines totally unsuited to meeting the demands of the modern battlefield.

Approximate figures of Japanese tank and armoured fighting vehicle production 1931–1945

Type 94 Tankette	823
Type 97 Tankette	616
Type 95 Light Tank	2,300
Type 92 Cavalry Tank	167
Type 89A Medium Tank	113
Type 89B Medium Tank	291
Type 97 Medium Tank	1,162
Type 97 Improved Medium Tank	930
Type 1 Medium Tank	170
Type 3 Medium Tank	144
Type 3 Gun Tank	31
Type 2 Amphibious Tank	182

Type 3 Amphibious Tank	12
Type 1 75 mm SP Gun	26
Type 1 105 mm SP Gun	54
Type 1 Armoured Personnel Transport	150–300

For a technologically advanced nation, Japan's total output of tanks and armoured fighting vehicles was miniscule when compared to America and the Soviet Union. Nazi Germany could not compete with the Allies in terms of overall production numbers and so implemented a policy of quality rather than quantity. A similar policy may have paid dividends for Japan had it been introduced in good time. Late war tank design showed a marked German influence, with designs such as the Chi-Nu and Chi-To being the qualitative equivalents of the American Sherman and Soviet T-34. It was Stalin who was once quoted as saying that, 'Quantity has a quality all its own.', and by 1944, the Soviet Union had both quality and quantity, notably the excellent T34-85 and IS-2 tanks. America too produced in quantity, and while the Sherman was often outgunned on European battlefields, it dominated the Pacific atolls and islands.

On the battlefields, Japan had neither quantity nor quality. The tanks that were committed to combat were in the main obsolete models which were totally outclassed by enemy models which had themselves been surpassed in terms of quality by the German panzers. When Japanese industry finally got around to turning out quality tanks, they were produced far too late, and in a piecemeal fashion which meant that they had to be reserved for homeland defence. The production problems which plagued Japanese tank design and manufacture were a result of conservatism, conceit, shifting priorities, and the strangulation of maritime trade by the American naval blockade.

Admiral Isoroku Yamamoto had risked his life to prevent war with America. More than anyone, he knew that Japan's limited industrial capacity could not compete with the vast economic superstate. It was somewhat ironic therefore that he was placed in the position of being the architect of the Pacific War by his own government. In a letter to a friend, he wrote, 'What a strange position I find myself in, having been assigned the mission diametrically opposed to my own personal opinion. Alas, is that fate?' In a letter to Admiral Nagano, he expressed his views without restraint by saying, 'We must not fight a war with so little chance of success.' He was absolutely correct, in that Japan could not produce aircraft, ships, artillery and tanks in quantity. Something had to give, and as the war in the Pacific was fought largely at sea and in the air, the production of tanks was sacrificed in favour of aircraft and ships.

Appendix 10
Tank Guns

Type 94 37 mm tank gun

This tank gun was the main armament for Japan's most numerous tank; the light Ha-Go which saw service throughout the war. The gun was mounted in the tank turret at approximately its centre of gravity. The main traverse of the gun was obtained by rotating the turret, although the gimbal mounting with vertical trunnions gave it a limited degree of free traverse. This obsolete gun had very limited combat value as it proved wholly incapable of making any impression on the Allied tanks encountered on the battlefield.

Calibre: 37 mm (1.46 in)
Barrel length: 1,850 mm (72.8 in)
Elevation: minus 10 to plus 25 degrees
Muzzle velocity: 579.1 m^2 (1,900 f^2)
Penetration: 35.5 mm (1.4 in) at 274 m

Type 90 57 mm tank gun

The Type 90 57 mm tank gun was mounted in the Type 89A & 89B medium tanks with some success. The decision to mount the same gun in the more modern Chi-Ha was according to Tomio Hara rather unfortunate as 'the splendid imposing figure of the Type 97 medium tank was unbalanced with a short barrelled 57 mm gun.' Hara's comment is not aimed primarily at the aesthetic features of the tank, but rather the missed opportunity of mounting a heavier gun on what turned out to be a splendid weapons platform. The Type 90 was a short-barrelled low-velocity tank gun which was essentially an infantry support weapon.

Calibre: 57 mm (2.24 in)
Barrel length: 1046.4 mm (41.2 in)
Elevation: minus 15 to plus 20 degrees
Muzzle velocity: 355.3 m^2 (1,166 f^2)
Penetration: 25 mm (0.98 in) at 1,000 m

The later Type 97 57 mm tank gun was also installed in the Chi-Ha. The muzzle velocity of this weapon was 420 m^2, giving it greater penetrating power.

Type 1 47 mm tank gun

Japanese pride and overconfidence was a significant factor in the failure to provide adequate armament for the nation's tank forces. This hubristic attitude inevitably led to nemesis which came in the form of General Zhukov's massed BT-5 and BT-7 tanks at Nomonhan in 1939. This shattering defeat directly led to the development of the 47 mm anti-tank gun. Designed specifically to counter the Soviet 45 mm tank gun, the Type 1 47 mm represented a great improvement on previous models. It was also the first completely indigenous anti-tank gun produced in Japan. In combat situations the Type 1 47 mm gun performed reasonably well, giving the 'improved' Shinhoto Chi-Ha on which it was mounted a fighting chance against heavier enemy tanks. In tests conducted by the U.S. Marines on Okinawa, the armour-piercing rounds were unable to make any impression on the glacis of a M4A6 Sherman, but penetrated 'all other parts at all ranges'. While still lagging behind modern world standards, the by no means negligible penetrating power of the new gun was put to good use in close-range ambushes.

Calibre: 47 mm (1.85 in)
Barrel length: 2,273 mm (7 ft 4.6 in)
Elevation: minus 15 to plus 20 degrees
Muzzle velocity: 810 m² (2,700 f²)
Penetration: 55 mm (2.2 in) at 100 m, 40 mm (1.6 in) at 500 m, 30 mm (1.2 in) at 1,000 m

Type 3 75 mm tank gun
The Type 3 75 mm tank gun was based on the Type 90 field gun which in turn was loosely based on the French Schneider-Creusot 85 mm artillery piece. The Type 3 75 mm gun was the main armament in the Chi-Nu medium tank and the Ho-Ni III gun tank. Had this more powerful gun been available earlier, Japanese tanks in the Pacific theatre would have been able to operate more in the open, perhaps even operating in the 'roving fire brigade' role envisioned by Colonel Nishi.

Calibre: 75 mm (3.0 in)
Barrel length: 2,865 mm (9 ft 4.2 in)
Elevation: minus 10 to plus 25 degrees
Muzzle velocity: 680 m² (2,200 f²)
Penetration: 90 mm (3.5 in) at 100 m, 65 mm (2.6 in) at 1,000 m

Appendix 11
Communications

Japan's post-war economic boom was largely characterised by the large-scale manufacture of high quality electronics products. In Britain, Japanese radios and Hi-Fi systems could be found in almost every home, their relative cheapness and high quality producing the impression that mass production had long been mastered in the land of the rising sun. In reality, nothing could have been further than the truth. Prior to 1945, the research and development of electronics was still largely in the hands of a small number of amateur inventor-entrepreneurs who toiled away in their miniscule garage-factories. Nonetheless, this select group was still able to make some valuable contributions towards the eventual creation of a modern electronics industry. One notable success was that of T. Takei and Y. Kato of the Tokyo Institute of Technology who in 1931 developed ferrite, a material that was later used in magnetic cores for high-frequency coils and transformers. Having noted these successes, both the government and the military authorities began to take a keen interest in radio. Despite this, the manufacturing of electronic components remained very much a cottage industry.

During the war years, both the Japanese Army and Navy actively promoted research into military communications. Collaborative projects with universities, Tokyo's Electro technical Laboratory, and the Japan Broadcasting Corporation Research Laboratory produced some positive results. For the military, the problem lay in translating these results into finished products as big business showed little interest in a highly labour-intensive process that failed to promise sufficient returns. Consequently, the wartime production of military grade communications equipment remained a piecemeal process which could only supply a very limited numbers of sets.

Shortages of military sets meant that, prior to 1943, 'only the tanks of regimental, company and platoon commanders were equipped with radios.' The situation improved slightly thereafter, but limited production of Type 94, Mk 4, Type 96 Mk 4 and Type 3 radio sets meant that flag signalling remained the main means of communication at platoon level. Flag signalling could of course not be used in the hours of darkness. For operations conducted during the night, coloured flares were sometimes used to transmit orders. These primitive methods were not suited to a modern battlefield as conditions often rendered them impracticable. In such circumstances, individual tank commanders were reduced to simply mimicking the actions of the platoon leader's tank.

Some of the Japanese radio sets captured by the Americans underwent a technical assessment in order to gauge their effectiveness. A January 1945 technical manual entitled *Japanese Radio Communications and Radio Intelligence* provides tangible evidence regarding the quality of the equipment available to Japanese tank commanders:

> Japanese radio materiel has varied from poor to excellent. All the early equipment captured has shown both poor design and construction and appeared to be several years behind American standards. The last few pieces

of equipment to fall into our hands have shown marked improvement in these respects.

Some materiel manufactured late in 1943, for example the airborne Type 3 Air Mk 1, and two vehicular sets TTK Model 147B and TM Model 305C have the latest features of electrical design and show real excellence of construction. Their main features are comparable to the latest American models.

In outward appearances, Japanese radios are neat and modern-looking. They are light weight, require a minimum of space and are easy to transport. Many are obviously copied from leading types manufactured by the United States, Britain or Germany.

The enemy has taken considerable pains to build radios which will withstand field conditions without need of servicing. The Naval Research Laboratory in Washington, commenting on a portable radio transmitter and receiver states. '… this set is very well constructed and its ruggedness, simplicity, and general excellence of design is worthy of note.' However, the article goes on to say, '… no fungus protection or weatherproofing is detectable.' This technical manual declares that the majority of Japanese radios studied are similarly lacking in weatherproofing of any kind. Japanese radios are apparently not built to withstand fungus or extreme humidity.

Another shortcoming of Japanese radios is the fact that they are in general extremely difficult to service. This feature is perhaps a by-product of the haste with which Japanese engineers have copied features from foreign-built radios. In some instances, entire back and front sections of the transmitter or receiver must be completely removed in order to repair one damaged part. Lack of trained personnel has also apparently affected Japanese radio maintenance….

The radio tubes manufactured by Japan at the present time are by and large inferior to our own. Japanese have in the past copied our tube designs and are continuing to do so.

As mentioned above, Japanese radio and electrical engineers have made remarkable strides recently towards the improvement of their apparatus. Generally speaking, Japanese radio sets have lagged several years behind those of America, Britain and Germany. However, since the outbreak of the war, Japan has captured large quantities of American radio gear and has made good use of its design. It should be remembered that the efficiency of any radio equipment varies widely with such factors as the skill of the operator, the frequency used, atmospheric conditions, sun-spot activity, and countless others. From the materiel point of view, however, it seems possible that Japan is approaching reasonably close to the quality of American equipment.

This rather chauvinistic and patronising report does at least acknowledge that the quality of Japanese radio equipment had improved. While the quality of radio sets may have improved, producing sets in sufficient quantity remained an issue, and it was not until very late in the war that tank models such as the Type 1 Chi-He medium tank had radios fitted as standard. The benefits of more effective communications were hardly felt on the battlefield as nearly all later tank models were reserved for home defence. As a consequence, communication between individual tanks and between tanks and higher command remained a problematic issue until the end of the war.

Appendix 12
Maintenance

The Japanese High Command was greatly impressed by German successes with their panzer arm and so not surprisingly sought to emulate them with similar tank formations of their own. In the event, the plan to recreate German successes was crippled from the start. Japanese planners failed to comprehend the enormous logistical strain which modern tank formations created. Industry was able to ease the strain to some degree by creating an excellent system of interchangeable parts and components. For example, some four and six cylinder engines were designed to utilise the same size cylinders, pistons, rings and rods. While the creation of interchangeable parts served to ease the strains on logistical services to some degree, intractable maintenance and supply problems continued to plague armoured and motorised units.

The maintenance of tanks in the field was carried out by company, regimental, and divisional units whose personnel were far more adept at maintaining wheeled transport than heavy armour. During the campaign in New Guinea their skills were put to the test as they had their hands full dealing with tyre shortages, poor springs, and the bad roads which shook the Japanese lorries to pieces. This is hardly surprising as Japan failed to produce a truck anywhere near as powerful and rugged as the famed American two-and-a-half-ton lorry produced by General Motors.

Throughout the war, the Izuzu Type 94 lorry formed the backbone of Japanese field maintenance units. Regimental maintenance companies were equipped with Type 94 repair lorries which carried a lathe, drill press, cutter, power generator and a selection of tools. This equipment enabled the maintenance section to carry out minor repairs in the field. Tank crews were themselves responsible for carrying out daily routine maintenance. This echelon system of maintenance was not always adhered to, with the inevitable consequence that attempts by unqualified personnel to make more complex repairs resulted in ruined valuable equipment.

The main issue bedevilling maintenance was a lack of specialised equipment. This situation was never resolved, and as Japan prepared to meet the anticipated American invasion, the tank regiments of the 1st Tank Division could only call on three light repair lorries and eight cargo lorries. The 4th Tank Division fared even worse, with each regiment only being able to muster a single light repair lorry and ten cargo lorries. It is highly doubtful whether this 'nominal' level of maintenance could have met the regiment's basic requirements for supplies and spare parts.

Appendix 13
Tank Crews

In Japan, the roaring nineteen-twenties were known as 'supiido no jidai' (the age of speed). This phrase reflected a sense of social change which promised a more modern, enlightened and liberated society. It was also a time in which the emerging urban society keenly followed the development of modern modes of communication and transportation. Movement became synonymous with life in the fast growing townships and cities. Cars soon began to dominate the streets as more and more people succumbed to the persuasive advertisements which guaranteed excitement and independence.

In Kyoto (Japan's fifth largest city) Ōzawa Enterprises employed the stunt of hiring a geisha to be their 'Chevrolet Girl.' This utilisation of American style advertising methods paid off handsomely for the Japanese agent for General Motors with 227 cars being sold in Kyoto alone between November 1927 and March 1928. More cars meant more motorists, and soon the Association of Automobile Drivers was providing advice and assistance to both new and more experienced drivers in ever increasing numbers. Learners could purchase a 'teach yourself' guide or attend a driving school such as the one at Ōmiya Shimabara in Kyoto. Driving became popular among middle-class 'Mobo's' (Modern Boys) who were characterised by their bell-bottom trousers, floppy tie, coloured shirt, and Harold-Lloyd style spectacles. Young women also took to the wheel, particularly 'Moga's' (Modern Girls) who emulated the flapper fashions and attitudes currently fashionable in America.

Meanwhile, in Tokyo, the police examined 55,700 applicants for driving licences in 1930. Of the 16,841 approved, many were young men. This trend was seen throughout the country, and as the first tank units were established, this pool of young men represented a valuable resource. Tank crews were selected from among those enlisted recruits who held a driving licence. The next tier was chosen from among those whose education indicated an understanding of the principles of mechanisation. This degree of elitism contrasted sharply with the Soviet Union where having driven a tractor on a collective farm was regarded as ample qualification.

Recruits to the tank arm undertook four months training with regiments during which time they learned the basics of the roles of driver, gunner, radio operator, and mechanic. Depending on the recruit's aptitude, they were then assigned to a specific role for more advanced training. Driver training usually took approximately one month, after which the recruit could drive both cars and tanks to a basic standard. The remainder of their training was taken up with gunnery practice, radio operation, flag signalling, mechanics and maintenance.

Holding a driving licence did not necessarily indicate any knowledge of mechanics. For this reason, basic training often started with lectures and demonstrations which covered the rudiments of the internal combustion engine. The majority of recruits to the tank arm wanted to earn their laurels in the heat of battle. For them, there was no honour or kudos attached to the servicing of tanks in the rear. Consequently, there was a chronic shortage of skilled mechanics, and despite efforts to recruit more, the problem was never fully resolved. Tankers were seen as mavericks, the knights-errant in an Army which still valued traditionalism. For the young well-educated recruits, their 'otherness' was an attraction in itself. They saw themselves as pioneers in a world in which military technology was fast evolving.

Appendix 14
Uniforms and Equipment

Tank crews were supplied with a one-piece coverall manufactured from a material similar to that used in the summer cotton uniform. The greyish-green coloured coverall buttoned up at the front (the buttons were concealed to prevent snagging on equipment) and featured a turn-down collar and a left-sided breast pocket. A fur-lined version was produced for tankers posted to Manchuria where the winters were notoriously harsh. This version featured a fur collar and additional chest and thigh pockets. Headgear largely consisted of the Type 92 tanker's helmet which was covered in canvas dyed the same colour as the standard coveralls. When not in combat, many tank crews preferred to wear their forage caps. A winter version of the tanker's helmet was also produced to compliment the fur-lined coverall. This fur-lined, leather covered version proved popular with crews as it provided additional protection as well as warmth.

For close protection, tank crews were issued with Type 94 Nambu 8 mm semi-automatic pistols. Some crews also carried a number of Type 38 Arisaka

6.5 mm carbines and Type 97 hand grenades as they were particularly useful when carrying out a reconnaissance on foot.

Some tank officers elected to take their swords with them, thus providing living proof of the tensions between traditionalism and modernism which characterised the Japanese Army.

Appendix 15
Tank Schools

The Chiba Tank School
This tank school was founded in 1936 at Narashino, located eastwards of Tokyo in the Chiba Prefecture. Originally, it was simply known as the 'Army Tank School.' In 1940 it changed its name to the 'Chiba Tank School' following the establishment of a second training facility at Kungchuling in the puppet state of Manchukuo. The Chiba Tank School trained officers and NCOs for the tank arm, and following a six month course, the successful candidates graduated and were then posted to their respective regiments.

The Siping Tank School
In 1942, the Chiba Tank School moved from Kungchuling to Siping. Following this move the name of the tank school was changed accordingly. As the tank school at Siping offered more space for manoeuvres, the training of drivers and gunners was allocated to this site. Because of its proximity to the Soviet–Manchurian border, this school focused on the armoured tactics needed to counter the Soviet threat.

The Army Cavalry School
After the First World War, Japan began the process of modernising its Army. In October 1918, the Army purchased a single British Mark IV tank for evaluation purposes. The following year, the decision was made to procure additional tanks for further evaluation and the initial training of tank crews. The British Medium A Whippet tanks and French FT tanks formed the nucleus of the first Japanese tank units which were formed in 1925. Some of the tank crews were trained at the Army Cavalry School located in the Chiba Prefecture. With the coming of increasing mechanisation, horsemanship training at the school ceased in 1937. The school then focused entirely on training light-tank and tankette crews in the art of reconnaissance.

The Fujinomiya Youth Tank School
In 1942, the sections of the tank school at Chiba which had focused on the training of young NCOs transferred to Fujinomiya, situated at the foot of

Mount Fuji in the Shizuoka Prefecture. During the last year of the war, the activities of youth military training schools became more and more important as 'much of the burden of defence was clearly going to fall upon the small but strong shoulders of Japan's youth.' The trainees of the Fujinomiya Youth Tank School featured in a late war edition of the *Photographic Weekly Report* (PWR) magazine. The lead article read, 'Suppressing their desire to be at the front, the youth tank crews undergo hard training. Today, from between the clouds, the sacred peak of Mount Fuji watches over these young men.' Following the loss of Saipan, PWR devoted many lead articles to the military training of adolescents.

Appendix 16
Tank Commander Kojiro Nishizumi and the Japanese propaganda machine

Kojiro Nishizumi was immortalised in Kenzaburo Yoshimura's 1940 propaganda film *Tank Commander Nishizumi*. After graduating from military academy in 1934, Nishizumi served as an infantry officer in Manchuria. Following his return to Japan he trained with the 2nd Tank Regiment in Narashino. He became the leader of a tank platoon in the 5th Tank Battalion and very quickly earned the trust and respect of the men under his command. As Japanese forces closed in on Nanking in 1938, he was wounded several times, but insisted on staying at the front with his men. The intensity of the fighting was etched on Nishizumi's Type 89 I-Go tank which bore the scars of over 1,300 bullet strikes. During the Battle of Hsuchou in May 1938, this brave soldier's luck finally ran out when he was shot and killed when carrying out a reconnaissance on foot.

In Tokyo, the Army Ministry was eager to uphold fallen soldiers as heroes in order to rally the home front. A major effort was made to portray Nishizumi as a 'military god' through a series of lectures and exhibitions. In December 1938, Tokyo's *Asahi Shinbun* newspaper dubbed 'Tank Commander Nishizumi' a 'shōwa military god.' This hyperbole was then taken a step further by the noted writer Kikuchi Kan who penned a very flattering biography that was later serialised in the *Osaka Mainichi Shinbun*. In November 1940, Shōchiku Studios released a feature film endorsed by the Army entitled 'The Legend of Tank Commander Nishizumi.' The film won praise from Captain Tatsuo Kobota, who wrote in the *Sutā* magazine that the tank was now in the eyes of the public as important as the aeroplane in the prosecution of modern warfare.

Ken Uehara, the actor chosen to portray Nishizumi was best known for playing the romantic leads and characters with a softer side in films such as

What did the lady forget? Notwithstanding, he succeeded in bringing a high degree of authenticity to his portrayal of Nishizumi, even utilising his father-in-law's military sword as a prop. The battle scenes in the film won particular praise from Kobota who wrote that, 'It was truly amazing how they did not even make one mistake. The result of their training was battle scenes the likes of which have not been seen even in a news film.' Uehara's acting was also praised for portraying a man who was recognised as 'the flower of modern warfare.' Inevitably, the film was a box office smash, though not everyone was bowled over, the *Tokyo Asahi* film critic opining that 'the tank seemed to be more like the film's main character.' Perhaps this was true to a point. Whatever the merits of this particular film, it certainly succeeded in raising the profile of the tank arm in the public consciousness.

Bibliography

Books and Journals

BOER, P, C., *The Loss of Java: The Final Battles for the possession of Java fought by Allied Air, Naval and Land Forces in the period 18 February–7 March 1942* (NUS Press 2011)

BRIDGE, C., *British and Japanese Military Leadership* (John Wiley & Sons 2010)

CRAIG, W., *The Fall of Japan* (London: Pan Books Ltd 1968)

DICKINSON, F. R., *World War I and the Triumph of a New Japan 1919–1930* (Cambridge University Press 2013)

DOERR, P. W., *The Changkufeng/Lake Khasan Incident of 1938: British Intelligence on Soviet and Japanese Military Performance* (Intelligence and National Security, Vol. 5, Issue 3, 1990)

DREA, E. J., *Japa's Imperial Army: Its Rise and Fall, 1853–1945* (University Press of Kansas 2009)

EALEY, M., *An August Storm: The Soviet-Japan Endgame in the Pacific War* (The Asia Pacific Journal, February 2006, Volume 4, Issue 2)

EARHART, D. C., *Certain Victory: Images of World War II in the Japanese Media* (Routledge 2015)

ELPHICK, P., *Singapore: The Pregnable Fortress* (London: Coronet 1995)

FARRELL, B. P., *The Defence and Fall of Singapore 1940–1942* (Stroud: Tempus 2006)

Ford, D., *US Assessments of Japanese ground warfare tactics and the Army's campaigns in the Pacific theaters, 1943-45: lessons learned and methods applied* (War in History, Vol. 16, Issue 3, July 2009)

GILBERT, O. E., *The Marine Corps Tank Collection* (Open Road Media 2018)

GLANTZ, D., *August Storm: The Soviet Strategic Offensive in Manchuria* (Combat Studies Institute, Fort Leavenworth 1983)

GOLDMAN, S. D., *Nomonhan 1939: The Red Army's Victory That Shaped WWII* (National Institute Press 2012)

GREEN, M., *Axis Tanks of the Second World War* (Pen & Sword 2017)

GUSTAVSSON, H., *Sino-Japanese Air War: The Longest Struggle* (Fonthill Media 2017)

HALLAS, J. H., *Saipan: The Battle That Doomed Japan in World War II* (Rowman & Littlefield 2019)

HARRIES, M., and HARRIES, S., *Soldiers of the Sun* (Heinemann 1991)

HASLAM, J., *Frontier Fighting: Lake Khasan (1938) and Khalkin-Gol (1939)* (Springer 1992)

HASEGAWA, T., *Racing the Enemy: Stalin, Truman, and the surrender of Japan* (Harvard University Press 2009)

HASTINGS, M., *Nemesis: The Battle for Japan 1944–45* (Harper Perennial 2007)

HIROAKI, K., *the Battle of Lake Khasan Reconsidered* (The Journal of Slavic Studies, Vol. 29, Issue 1, 2016)

HIXTON, W. L., *The American Experience in World War II: Pearl Harbor in History and Memory* (Taylor & Francis 2003)

HORIE, Y., and ELDRIDGE, R. D. and TATUM C. W. (eds) *Fighting Spirit: The Memoirs of Major Yoshitaka Horie and the Battle of Iwo Jima* (Naval Institute Press 2011)

HOUGH, F. O., *The Assault on Peleliu* (Historical Division, Headquarters U.S. Marine Corps 1950)

KATOCH, H. S., *The Battle of Imphal March—July 1944* (Journal of Defence Studies, Vol. 8, No. 3, 2014)

KIKUOKA, M. T., *Changkufeng Incident: A Study in Soviet-Japanese Conflict, 1938* (Rowman & Littlefield 1988)

KIND, D., *A Tomb Called Iwo Jima: Firsthand Accounts From Japanese Survivors* (Pacific Press 2014)

KOWNER, R., *When Economics, Strategy, and Racial Ideology Meet : Inter-Axis connections in the wartime Indian Ocean,* (Journal of Global History, Vol. 12, Issue 2, July 2017)

MANSOOR, P. R., and MURRAY, W., eds., *The Culture of Military Organisations* (Cambridge University Press 2019)

MILLER, J., *Guadalcanal: The First Offensive Volume 2, Part 3* (Historical Division, Department of the Army 1949)

NESS, L., *Rikugun—Guide to Japanese Ground Forces 1937–1945 Volume 1: Tactical Organisation of Imperial Japanese Army & Navy Ground Forces* (Helion & Company Ltd 2014)

NESS, L., *Rikugun—Guide to Japanese Ground Forces 1937–1945 Volume 2: Weapons of the Imperial Japanese Army & Navy Ground Forces* (Helion & Company Ltd 2015)

NESS, L., and SHIH, B., *Kangzhan: Guide to Chinese Ground Forces 1937–45* (Helion 2016)

PEATTIE, M., DREA, E., and VAN DE VEN, H., eds, *The Battle for China: Essays on the Military History of the Sino-Japanese War of 1937–1945* (Stanford University Press 2011)

ROTTMAN, G. L., and TAKIZAWA, A., *World War II Japanese Tank Tactics* (Osprey Publishing Ltd 2008)

SMITH, C., *Singapore Burning* (London: Penguin 2006)

STAHL, D. C., *The Burdens of Survival: Ōoka Shōhei's Writings on the Pacific War* (University of Hawaii 2003)

STILLE, M., *Guadalcanal 1942–43: America's First Victory on the Road to Tokyo* (Bloomsbury Publishing 2015)

SUNOO, H. H., *Japanese Militarism: Past and Present* (Chicago: Nelson Hall 1975)

TAKAHASHI, Y., *A Network of Tinkerers: The Advent of the Radio and Television Receiver Industry in Japan* (Technology and Culture, Vol. 41, No. 3, July 2000)

Toland, J., *Rising Sun* (Random House 1970)

YAHARA, H., *The Battle for Okinawa: A Japanese Officers Eyewitness Account of the Last Great Campaign of World War II* (John Wiley & Sons, Inc. 1995)

YOUNG, K. H., *The Nomonhan Incident: Imperial Japan and the Soviet Union* (Monumenta Nipponica, Vol. 22, No. 1/2, 1967)

ZALOGA, S., *Armoured Champion: The Top Tanks of World War II* (Stackpole Books 2015)

ZALOGA, S., *Japanese Tanks 1939–45* (Osprey Publishing Ltd 2007)

Reports

HOFFMAN, C. W., *Saipan: The Beginning of the End* (Historical Division, U.S. Marine Corps, 1950)

WAELDE, R., *The Experience of the Japanese-Chinese War and the Spanish Civil War for the development of the German 'Blitzkrieg Doctrine' and its lessons for the Transformation process* (School of Advanced Military Studies, U.S. Army Command and General Staff College, Fort Leavenworth, Kansas, 2003)

Official Publications

Burma Operations Record—15th Army Operations in the Imphal Area and Withdrawal to Northern Burma (Headquarters United States Army Japan, Distributed by the Office of the Chief of Military History, Department of the Army, 1957)

Campaign in the Marianas (Center of Military History, United States Army, 1993)

Enemy Japan (United States War Information Office, 1945)

Japanese Monograph No. 45—History of the Imperial General Headquarters (Army Section, Assistant Chief of Staff, G3, Foreign Histories Division, Headquarters United States Army, Japan, 1959)

Japanese Tank and Antitank Warfare: Special Series No. 34 (Military Intelligence Division, War Department, Washington DC, 1945)

Study of Japanese Defence at Betio Island: Part 1—Fortifications and Weapons (Intelligence Section, 2nd Marine Division, 1943)